CAN I
REALLY
BELIEVE?

CAN I REALLY BELIEVE?

Howard F. Vos

WORLD
PUBLISHING

CONTENTS

ABBREVIATIONS OF BIBLE VERSIONS

KJV: The King James Version
NASB: The New American Standard Bible
NIV: The New International Version
NJB: The New Jerusalem Bible
NKJV: The New King James Version
RSV: The Revised Standard Version

A BEGINNING WORD

The contemporary Christian has a serious problem. And so does the non-Christian who seeks truth. The modern mind says that knowledge must pass the tests of reason and/or experimentation and that religious truth cannot be as certainly known as scientific truth. In fact, modern thinkers often say that science and technology are based on facts; religion is a matter of opinion or faith. Is a Christian's hope for time and eternity based on the mere opinion of a certain group of church leaders? And do those who call themselves Christians have to put aside the exercise of their minds when they follow their Christian convictions?

The argument of this book is that Christianity is based not merely on faith but on facts as well—lots of facts. Furthermore, the Christian is strongest who engages the mind fully in the understanding and defense of the faith. The defense presented here primarily uses information gleaned from research in history and archaeology but also involves philosophical argumentation and biblical understanding.

The approach taken is a very personal one. It tackles questions that those who seek truth often need to have answered in order to accept the Christian faith. Additionally, it deals with questions that critics frequently throw out to confuse Christians.

To begin with, as we read the Bible we come across dramatic stories that we heard in Sunday school. Or if we never went to church in our youth, we knew about those stories from music that we have heard or literature that we have read or paintings that we have seen—stories like the fall of the walls of Jericho, the Israelites' crossing the Red Sea, or the destruction of Sodom and Gomorrah. At a certain point in our development, we may wonder if those events ever took place; were they even plausible? Or were they good stories like those that Arabs tell around the campfire today in the Near East, as some modern theologians occasionally charge. In other words, can we believe in the historical trustworthiness of the Bible?

We also often wonder about how accurate the text of the Bible really is. After all, it is hard to be sure about the accuracy of passages in Plato or Aristotle or even Chaucer or Shakespeare; and the Bible was written long before any of that literature. Have passages in the Bible been corrupted like other ancient literature that was copied by hand over the centuries before the invention of printing?

But even if we can show that the Bible has been wonderfully preserved down through the ages, how can we know that the Bible is inspired? That it is God's message to us? And how can we defend the idea of the miraculous in a materialistic age when it is often fashionable to deny miracles?

Then, while most of us have no problem accepting the fact that Jesus lived on earth, athiests sometimes deny that. How can we support our belief? Although it is not hard to demonstrate that Jesus really did live on earth, it is much more difficult to show that He was truly God. It is an equally big order to make a case for His resurrection from the dead. But it is absolutely necessary to do so because, as the apostle Paul declared, if Christ is not risen, our preaching is in vain and our faith is without foundation (1 Corinthians 15:4).

One major question remains—one that humanity in general and even Christians on their most frustrating days may ask: Does God really exist?

As we struggle with all these questions, we are not forced to depend only on a nebulous faith, some hazy or indistinct or dimly realized hope. Hebrews 11:1 speaks of something more tangible. The English versions describe faith as an "assurance" or "substance" of things hoped for; in the Greek original, the term has the significance of a title deed to property. In other words, one's faith is some sort of "guarantee" (NJB) of our inheritance.

As we live our lives at the end of the twentieth century, we can also enter into all the benefits of the research of defenders of the faith who draw from the various branches of knowledge to help answer the questions we have raised. So, with great appreciation for all the information now available to bolster our faith, we engage in this study of the defense of the faith. Understandably our study is brief and our efforts very selective. It is impossible here to deal with all the questions facing modern Christians as they read their Bibles, and as they live life. A few additional helpful books appear in a list at the end of this study.

Chapter 1

CAN I REALLY BELIEVE THE STORIES OF THE BIBLE?

As the professor began his lecture on Hebrew literature, he immediately grabbed my attention. Full of enthusiasm for his subject, he exclaimed, "These Old Testament stories are wonderful; I love them! They're just like the stories that Arabs tell around the campfire today over in the Near East." Then he continued, "It doesn't matter whether they really happened. Just as stories from Homer's *Iliad* and *Odyssey* and other ancient works are great literature and have inspired masterpieces of painting, sculpture, music or literature, so have these biblical stories."

In my mind I had to disagree with him totally. It is important that biblical events did occur as they are reported. If the Bible is shot through with myth and historical and scientific error, then it is harder for us to accept the truth of its doctrinal message. After a while we may question whether any of the Bible should command our respect.

To be sure, Bible stories do make nice entertainment and instruction for the Sunday-school child. They also furnish good subject matter for paintings, dramas, musicals, and literary pieces, but they don't need to be fiction to produce a significant artistic impact. And it could be devastating for Sunday-school children to discover on growing older that the stories they had believed so fervently never happened. They might conclude that religious leaders had tricked them and wonder whom and what to believe now. Of course all of us need to know that we can trust the historical content of the Bible whether we are seekers after God or believers confronted by critics who try to destroy the faith. To head off loss of faith over alleged historical error or fiction in the Bible, let us look at some of the better-known stories of the Old Testament to discover evidence that they actually happened, or at least are plausible.

ABRAHAM AND HIS HOMETOWN OF UR

One of the greatest heroes of the Old Testament is Abraham, and we hear early in childhood about how God called Abraham from Ur in southern Iraq to follow Him by faith (Genesis 11:31–12:5; Acts 7:2–4). It is understandable that we should learn about Abraham early on, because he is connected with all three of the world's great monotheistic religions. He was the ancestor of the Jews through Sarah and of the Arabs (Muslims) through Hagar. And he holds a special place in Christianity as an example of salvation by faith and as the ancestor of Christ, through whom all Christians obtain their salvation.

For the average reader of the Bible today, God's command that Abraham leave Ur and go to a land that God would show him was "no big deal." After all, did not Abraham and his family live in tents? Were they not simply being told to pick up and go elsewhere? And why make such a fuss over leaving an insignificant ancient village?

Modern research casts new light on this ancient story. As a result of the excavations by the British archaeologist, Sir C. Leonard Woolley at Ur from 1922 to 1934, as well as

12

on the basis of more recent research, we now know that Ur was a very sophisticated place in Abraham's day. It was a city-state of considerable size, in control of an empire that covered the entire Mesopotamian valley—roughly the size of the modern country of Iraq. The city-state had a population of about 360,000, according to Woolley, with about 25,000 within the walls of the city center.[1]

A highly developed commercial center, Ur had business houses that maintained representatives or salesmen along the Persian Gulf as well as throughout the Mesopotamian valley. These business people kept extensive records; large numbers of invoices, contracts, and bills of lading have been found in the ruins of the city. To their credit they used a fairly sophisticated double-entry bookkeeping system. Numerous schools also made education available to at least the upper classes, and math students knew how to extract square and cube roots and do simple exercises in geometry. As a matter of fact, the whole area of Mesopotamia was highly urbanized and quite sophisticated, and large numbers of nomads were not wandering hither and yon with their tents.

Abraham was a city dweller who, in the first stage of his journey after leaving Ur, traveled some five hundred miles to Haran, a city in northern Mesopotamia. When he left Haran at about age seventy-five and went to Canaan (Palestine), Abraham did have to resort to living in tents. So, as people count reputation or significance, it did mean something, in fact it meant a great deal, for him to leave Ur, the greatest city of the Near East at the time, to follow God by faith to some lesser place. It may not take much faith to

---

1 C. L. Woolley, *History of Mankind*, vol. 1 (New York: New American Library, 1965), 2:123–24. More recent scholars tend to reduce the population figure somewhat. C. L. Woolley wrote several books about Ur. One of the most useful is *Ur of the Chaldees*, revised by P. R. S. Moorey [London: Herbert Press, 1982]).

13

believe that God called Abraham from Ur, but modern discoveries help to show us what it meant for Abraham to leave this renown city. And they give a new sense of the reality of the biblical narrative as they enable us to walk down streets that Abraham may have trod, past business houses with which he may have had numerous dealings, and through the ruins of houses whose inhabitants he may have known.

In fact, far different from being merely a wandering nomad, Abraham may have been a merchant prince. As a case in point, when he bought the cave of Machpelah at Hebron as a burial place for his wife Sarah, he weighed out silver "current money with the merchant" (Genesis 23:16 KJV); he did not barter sheep or camels or other wealth for the land. Moreover, besides this reference, Genesis 13:2 and 24:35 mention that Abraham was rich in gold and silver.[2] Later in the patriarchal period we see this same involvement in business. The people of Shechem gave permission to Jacob's household to "dwell . . . and trade" and "get you possessions [real estate] therein" (Genesis 34:10 KJV). Subsequently, Joseph discussed with his brothers permission to trade in Egypt (Genesis 42:34).

Whether or not we accept the idea that Abraham was a merchant prince, he was a city dweller of considerable means. In fact, within ten or fifteen years after he arrived in Canaan, he had 318 armed retainers in his company (Genesis 14:14). Including the wives and children of these men, he must have led a company of over a thousand. Only a chief of great wealth and power could maintain such a

---

2 For a discussion of Abraham as a merchant prince, see Cyrus Gordon, "Abraham and the Merchants of Ura, *Journal of Near Eastern Studies* (January 1958): 28–30; William F. Albright, *Yahweh and the Gods of Canaan* (Garden City, N.Y.: Doubleday, 1968), 51, 62–73; David N. Freedman, "The Real Story of the Ebla Tablets," *Biblical Archaeologist* (December 1978): 158.

force—even conducting successful warfare with others classified as kings (*see* Genesis 14).

Several years after Abraham arrived in Canaan, God determined to destroy the sinful city of Sodom and its neighboring towns. This dramatic event is another story requiring investigation to determine the likelihood of its historicity.

THE DESTRUCTION OF SODOM AND GOMORRAH

The account of the destruction of Sodom and Gomorrah has served down through the centuries as a warning to those who engage in gross sin. But some skeptics feel that the Genesis narrative is a little too pat and too dramatic to have happened as reported: God "rained on Sodom and Gomorrah sulphur and fire out of heaven; and he overthrew those cities, and all the Plain. (Genesis 19:24–25 RSV). Such skeptics tend to smile and treat this as a nice story with a moral and ethical purpose.

In dealing with whether the destruction of Sodom and Gomorrah is true or not, it is important first to decide where Sodom and the other cities of the plain may have stood and then to discover if anything in that region seems to bear on, or tally with, the biblical account. In Scripture itself appear several indications leading to the conclusion that Sodom and Gomorrah were in the southern part of the Dead Sea region. Three references are particularly convincing. First, Genesis 14:10 (KJV)states that the battle between the four kings and the five was fought in the "vale of Siddim," which was "full of slime pits"—asphalt or bitumen wells. Bitumen has been and is found in considerable quantities around the Dead Sea, especially around the southern end.

Second, according to Genesis 19:20–23, Lot escaped from Sodom to nearby Zoar. William F. Albright pointed out that in Roman, Byzantine, and Arabic times there was a town of Zoar located at the south end of the Dead Sea. Since this site bears no evidence of occupation before the Christian period, Albright believed that the town of Abraham's day lies under the waters of the Dead Sea and that the name was transferred to the new town.[3] At least the name *Zoar* has long been applied to a town in that region.

Third, Genesis 14:3 states that the battle of the four kings and the five took place in the vale of Siddim, "which is the salt sea" (KJV). Presumably this parenthetical clause indicates that the Dead Sea subsequently overflowed the vale of Siddim. The first-century Jewish historian, Josephus, confirms the testimony of this biblical reference in saying that, with the disappearance of Sodom, the valley has become a lake, "the so-called Asphaltitis" (his name for the Dead Sea).[4]

That the water level of the Dead Sea has risen in modern times is confirmed by abundant evidence, not the least of which is the large number of dead trees standing in the water at the south end. Also, the road around the southern end of the sea has been under water since the end of the last century. Moreover, it is now known that a Roman road ran along the east side of the Dead Sea and across El Lisan ("the tongue" that juts into the sea from the eastern shore), connecting to the western shore (somewhere near Masada). So it must have been possible to ride or walk across that area of the Dead Sea in Roman times. Perhaps it should be noted that most of the southern part of the sea is only about twelve to fifteen feet deep and that the water level commonly rises at least two to three inches each year. The sea expands and contracts with climatic conditions, however. Presently it is contracting, partly as a result of the fact that Jordan River water flowing into it is being used for irrigation.

---

3 William F. Albright, *Archaeoloqy of Palestine and the Bible* (Cambridge, Mass.: American Schools of Oriental Research, 1974), 135.

4 *Antiquities* 1, 9.

Related to the Sodom and Gomorrah skepticism are discoveries at Bab edh-Dhra', a site located just east of El Lisan. This large fortified enclosure was believed to be a religious or festival site for nearby cities. Its cemetery is estimated to contain some five-hundred thousand burial sites and to have been used into the twenty-first century B.C.[5] The cessation of burials tallies roughly with the chronology for Abraham based on the Hebrew text, which puts the destruction of the cities of the plain at about 2075 B.C.

If we conclude that Sodom and the other cities of the plain were probably located at the south end of the Dead Sea, we must next find out if there is any hint in area conditions that there was once such a violent destruction as the book of Genesis indicates. Three ancient commentators give specific witness to the devastation of the area. The Greek geographer Strabo writing at the end of the first century B.C. concerning the area at the south end of the Dead Sea) mentioned ruined settlements, fissures in the ground, ashy soil, scorched rocks, and other evidences of a general destruction in the region. He attributed much of the destruction to earthquakes.

Josephus (end of the first century A.D.) described the burned-out appearance of the area and the remains of ruined cities. Writing about the same time, the Roman historian Tacitus attributed, as did Josephus, the destruction of the cities of the plain to bolts of lightning and described the burned-out appearance and the destruction of the fertility of the land. Parenthetically it should be observed that, according to the testimony of these men, apparently the land south of El Lisan was not entirely under water by A.D. 100. Other ancient writers spoke of the existence in the plain of asphalt seepage and boiling water that

---

5 A. Ben-Tor, "Bab Edh-Dhra'," *Encyclopedia of Archaeological Excavations in the Holy Land,*, ed. Michael Avi-Yonah, 1, 149–51 (Englewood Cliffs, N.J.: Prentice-Hall, 1975).

emitted foul odors. Great quantities of asphalt or bitumen appear in the Dead Sea region and continue to rise to the surface of the water.[6]

J. Penrose Harland of the University of North Carolina, who has made one of the most definitive studies of the destruction of these cities, reconstructs the story of the destruction as follows: "A great earthquake, perhaps accompanied by lightning, brought utter ruin and a terrible conflagration to Sodom and the other communities in the vicinity. The destructive fire may have been caused by the ignition of gases and seepage of asphalt emanating from the region, through lightning or the scattering of fires from hearths."[7] Harland also quotes extensively from a geological survey of the region by Frederick G. Clapp, who concluded that the "slime pits" were probably oil or bitumen seepages and held to the probability of the existence of natural gas in the area. Clapp further observed that seepage of semifluid petroleum may still be found near the south end of the Dead Sea.[8]

From all this discussion it is clear that there was an abundance of combustible material near these cities. And there is no reason to doubt the Genesis account of intense fire and smoke and the raining of fiery substance on the cities, possibly as a result of gas explosions that threw burning material into the air. Whether lightning touched off fire and explosions or whether earthquakes created a chain reaction need not concern us here. Genesis describes the catastrophe, and early geographers attest to it.

In answer to those who question whether the supernatural has been discounted in the foregoing discussion, it

---

6 For references to all these ancient writers, see J. Penrose Harland, "Sodom and Gomorrah," pt. 2, *Biblical Archaeologist* (September 1943): 44–47.

7 Ibid., 48.

8 Ibid., 49

should be observed that miracles sometimes involve secondary causes. Moreover, the time element is often the main feature in the miracle. In this case, God may have used an earthquake and lightning to set combustible materials on fire, *after adequate warning to Abraham and Lot, after Lot's escape from Sodom, and in complete accordance with a divine timetable.*

The vivid account of the destruction of Sodom and Gomorrah in Genesis 19 may be an eyewitness description written by Abraham himself. Commonly, the well-to-do in Ur in Abraham's day could read and write. If Abraham could not write, he was certainly wealthy enough to employ scribes to keep whatever accounts or compose whatever records he chose to produce. It is not at all necessary to believe either that Moses incorporated oral traditions in the early chapters of Genesis or that God had to reveal or dictate all the contents of these early chapters to him. Moses could have used historical accounts written by Abraham and others.

Long after Abraham's day, the Hebrews left Palestine for Egypt to escape a terrible drought and famine. In Egypt they were eventually reduced to slavery, and at the end of 430 years in the land of the Nile (Exodus 12:40) they fled in what is called the Exodus. The biblical account describes the ten plagues that preceded their flight, their crossing the Red Sea, and the drowning of the Egyptians who followed them.

THE CROSSING OF THE RED SEA

On the face of it, it seems preposterous to ask anyone to believe that the waters of the Red Sea parted for the Israelites as they fled from the Egyptians at the time of the Exodus and then closed behind them, drowning the pursuing Egyptians. Yet that is exactly what the Exodus narrative says, and even those who have never read the book of Exodus know the story. Exodus 14:21–22 tells specifically how it happened: "And the LORD swept the sea back by a strong east wind all night, and turned the sea into dry land, so the waters were divided. And the sons of Israel went through the midst of the sea on the dry land" (NASB).

Any discussion of this event must deal with the Exodus route. The usual view is that the Israelites went south from Goshen and crossed the Red Sea south of the modern port of Suez. An alternate view holds that they traveled east through the lakes, now part of the Suez Canal system. Those who hold this view tend to translate the Hebrew *yam sûph* (e. g., Exodus 13:18) as "Sea of Reeds" instead of "Red Sea." In either case, a miracle had to take place to part the waters and provide a dry path for the Israelites.

In this narrative, however, a look at all the evidence seems to dictate that *yam sûph* be translated "Red Sea." This is true, first, because the Greek translation of the Exodus narrative (the Septuagint) as well as Acts 7:36 and Hebrews 11:29, understand *yam sûph* to refer to the Red Sea. Second, Exodus 14:27 and 15:5, 8, 10 seem to require something larger than one of the lakes of the Suez region. Such expressions as "the sea returned to its full depth" (14:27 NKJV), and "they sank like lead in the mighty waters" (15:10 NKJV) do not easily apply to a lake—even a large one. Third, *yam sûph* in Exodus 10:19 would seemingly have to be more than the marshy lakes of the Suez region. In that instance a divinely ordered wind blew the locusts of the eighth plague from the entire land of Egypt into the Red Sea. A large lake or lakes could hardly have accommodated all the insects, but the Gulf of Suez is large enough to have destroyed the hordes of locusts and is properly placed for a northwest wind to blow them into its waters. Finally, in Numbers 14:25 *yam sûph* appears to refer to the Red Sea. Perhaps it is best, then, to conclude that the Hebrews journeyed southward to the west of the present canal system and crossed the Red Sea just south of the modern port of Suez.

If we conclude that the Israelites crossed the Red Sea, the modern mind then asks, "Could they have done so?" Bible believers and supernaturalists answer, "Yes." Others may shrug their shoulders. There the matter stood until recently, when Doron Nof, professor of oceanography at Florida State University, and Nathan Paldor, an expert in atmospheric science at Hebrew University in Jerusalem tackled the question. They were not trying to prove the accuracy of the Exodus narrative but merely sought to discover whether this crossing was scientifically plausible. Their research shows that strong winds in the region of the north end of the Red Sea (*see* Exodus 14:29) do indeed sometimes lower the water level and could have lowered the water level to the point of producing bare land, and they identify an undersea ridge that could have provided a temporary bridge for the Israelites to pass over.[9] So, it now seems scientifically justifiable to accept the Israelites' crossing of the Red Sea; the miracle of the event lies in the timing of proper atmospheric conditions just as the Israelites were ready to cross.

Forty years later, at the end of the wilderness wanderings, the Hebrews had subdued tribal groups east of the Jordan River and prepared to cross the river and attack the peoples of western Palestine. God gave Joshua specific instructions for crossing the Jordan and promised a dry path to the Israelite host.

THE CROSSING OF THE JORDAN

The Israelite's crossing of the Jordan does not require nearly as much faith to accept as does their crossing of the

9 See John N. Wilford, "Oceanographers Say Winds May Have Parted the Waters," *New York Times*, 15 March 1992; Doron Nof and Nathan Paldor, "Are There Oceanographic Explanations for the Israelites' Crossing of the Red Sea?," *Bulletin of the American Meteorological Society* (March 1992): 305–14.

Red Sea. Today the Jordan River near Jericho is an insignificant stream.[10]

But before much of its waters were used for irrigation, it was a substantial one-hundred-foot-wide barrier to those who sought entrance to Palestine. At the time of the year that the Israelites crossed, the river was at flood stage, thus imposing an even greater impediment.

God ordered the Israelites to prepare to enter Canaan. The priests were to carry the ark before the people; and as soon as the feet of the priests came to the water's edge, the Jordan would cease to flow (Joshua 3:13). The entire Israelite company then passed over on dry ground. Some have argued that the piled-up waters and the resultant dry path across the Jordan for all the Israelites to cross would have caused destructive flooding across the whole Jordan plain. Actually a careful reading of the Joshua narrative makes it clear that the path for a crossing was not narrow. The text says that the river was dammed up at Adam and Zarethan (3:16); Adam, the modern Damieh, is about eighteen miles north of Jericho. Since Jericho was close to ten miles north of the Dead Sea, the streambed for a distance of some twenty-five miles would have been dry, and the whole company of Israelites could quickly cross.

At least two datable blockages of the Jordan are known to have occurred near Damieh. In A.D. 1267 a mound on the west side of the river collapsed into it and dammed it up for sixteen hours.[11] Similarly, in 1927 a cliff fell into the river and blocked its flow for twenty-one-and-a-half hours.[12] Very

---

10 The current shrinkage of the Jordan does not eliminate the value of the river as a useful defense barrier for the modern state of Israel, however. Much of the riverbed lies in a deep gorge, and along the middle course of the river there stretches a virtually impenetrable thicket a mile or so wide.

11 John Garstang, *Joshua and Judges* (London: Constable, 1931), 136–137.

likely an earthquake was responsible for the obstruction of the Jordan in Joshua's day. Judges 5:4 says the earth "trembled" or "quaked" when the Israelites entered the land; and Psalm 114:3–4 (KJV) says, "Jordan was driven back. The mountains skipped like rams," probably a poetic description of an earthquake. The suggestion that an earthquake may have blocked the Jordan in Joshua's day does not eliminate a miracle from the narrative. The miracle in this case came with the timing; the waters ceased to flow precisely as priest's feet came to the water's edge. There is no reason to doubt that the Jordan River ceased to flow, as the Joshua narrative claims.

Soon after the Hebrews crossed the Jordan, they faced the daunting task of conquering a land inhabited by numerous peoples stronger than they (Numbers 13:31; Deuteronomy. 7:1), used to defending themselves with well-forged weapons, and protected by formidable fortifications—"cities walled to heaven" (Numbers 13:28; Deuteronomy 1:28; 3:5; 9:1 KJV and NKJV). The first bastion that faced them was the city of Jericho. There and elsewhere God intervened on behalf of the ill-equipped Hebrews and largely won the battle for them, causing the ramparts to collapse and paralyzing the inhabitants with fear as they heard how God had dried up the Red Sea and the Jordan before the advancing Israelites (Joshua 2:9–11; 5:1).

THE FALL OF THE WALLS OF JERICHO

The account of the fall of the walls of Jericho is one of the best-known stories of the Bible. Even those who have never read the book of Joshua have probably heard the words: "Joshua fit the battle of Jericho, and the walls come tumbling down" as found in the spiritual. As Joshua 6 tells it, the Hebrews were to march around the city once a day for six days and seven times on the seventh day, at which

---

12 Ibid., 137.

time they were to shout and the walls would fall down. Then they were to destroy everything in the city except Rahab and her family and metal objects that were to be dedicated to the tabernacle worship. The Hebrews obeyed and the city was destroyed as predicted.

Is the Joshua narrative just so much folklore and religious rhetoric or did the destruction of Jericho happen that way? In order to find an answer, we must turn to archaeology.

The first extensive excavation of Old Testament Jericho (Tell es-Sultan) occurred from 1907 to 1909, under the direction of Ernst Sellin and Carl Watzinger of the German Oriental Society. The usefulness of this expedition was limited because chronological systems were poorly understood at the time, but it did show that the city covered only about eight and one-half acres. Thus, it was possible for the Israelites to have marched around it once a day, or even seven times a day. Some, equating the amount of attention that is given to Jericho in the Old Testament with a great city like Babylon or Nineveh, believed that Jericho could not have been encircled as the biblical narrative indicates. But, the first excavation of Jericho, which revealed its size, removed that hindrance to faith.

The second archaeological expedition at Jericho was an English dig, led by John Garstang from 1930 to 1936. Garstang identified the wall of Joshua's day as a double wall on top of the mound on which the city was built and commented that the outer wall fell down the slope of the mound, and the inner wall collapsed into the space between the walls. Traces of intense fire appeared everywhere. He said that the walls fell outward so completely that attackers could easily climb over their ruins into the city.[13] Garstang also claimed that all evidence pointed to a fall of the city to the Israelites about 1400 B.C.

------

13 Ibid.145–46.

Kathleen Kenyon conducted the third major archaeological campaign at Jericho for the British School of Archaeology in Jerusalem (1952–58). She demonstrated that the wall on top of the mound that Garstang dated to Joshua's day belonged to the period 3000–2000 B.C. and could have had no connection with Joshua, and she dated the fall of the city some fifty years later than did Garstang.[14] There the matter lay until after Kenyon's death in 1978.

Her excavation reports, published posthumously at the end of the last decade, have received careful analysis by Bryant Wood, an archaeologist at the University of Toronto and a specialist on Jericho. Based on Kenyon's reports, Wood observes that there was a stone revetment surrounding the mound on which the town was built. On this revetment was a mud-brick wall. The revetment held in place a flat rampart, above which (higher up the slope) stood a second mud-brick wall that constituted Jericho's city wall proper. So, there were two concentric walls with houses in between (was one of them Rahab's?). Kenyon herself had discovered piles of bricks that had fallen down from the revetment wall surrounding the city and that would have enabled attackers to climb up into the city.[15] Moreover, in line with God's command not to take the city's goods, abundant and valuable supplies of grain turned up in the excavation.[16] Evidently the city did not fall as a result of a starvation siege, as was common in the ancient Near East. Stones, bricks, and timbers were found, blackened from a citywide fire, tallying with the biblical indication that the Israelites burned the city. On the basis of Kenyon's excavation reports, Wood also argued that all evidence pointed to an approximate 1400 B.C. date for the fall of the city.

---

14 Bryant G. Wood, "Did the Israelites Conquer Jericho?" *Biblical Archaeology* Review (March/April 1993): 50.

15 Ibid., 54.

16 Ibid., 56.

To summarize, Wood concludes that the walls of Jericho did indeed fall so attackers could climb up over the debris to burn the city but not to plunder it. He, like many others, believes it was an earthquake that triggered the destruction. Perhaps we can conclude this section in no better way than by quoting the headline of the *New York Times* article reporting on the posthumous analysis of Kenyon's work: "Believers Score in Battle Over the Battle of Jericho"[17]

After the conquest of the land, the period of the Judges, and the reigns of Saul and David (a period of well over three-hundred years) came the reign of Solomon.

THE GLORIES OF THE REIGN OF SOLOMON

Scripture and tradition both tend to glorify the reign of Solomon. A summary of the great achievements of his reign appears in 1 Kings 9–10. It includes the construction of the temple and his palace complex; the construction of a port at Ezion-gebber on the Red Sea and a merchant marine to use it; and fortifications at Jerusalem, Megiddo, Hazor, Gezer, and elsewhere. There is also reference to his commercial ventures, to his great wealth, and, especially, to his proverbial wisdom.

Critics and popular commentators have argued that Solomon's glory as portrayed in Scripture far exceeds the facts, and his kingdom could not have become a significant power among the great empires of the Middle East. They claim that the Babylonians, Assyrians, Egyptians, Persians, and others would have smothered him. When we examine the historical chronology, however, we discover that there was a power vacuum in the Middle East and eastern Mediterranean during the days of David and Solomon (1010–931 B.C.). The Hittite Empire of Asia Minor and Syria came to an end shortly after 1200 B.C. The great days of the Mycenean

---

17 John Noble Wilford, 22 February 1990, A8.

Greeks and the Egyptian Empire ceased by 1100 B.C. The Assyrians threatened to dominate Mesopotamia and Syria about 1100 B.C. and then slumped back into insignificance until about 900. The Old Babylonian Empire of Hammurabi had disappeared by 1550 B.C., and the Neo-Babylonian Empire of Nebuchadnezzar and his father did not begin to rise until about 625. The Persians did not begin to make their mark until after about 550.

Thus, it is clear that there was no great power in the vicinity to get in the way of Hebrew expansion in the days of David and Solomon. Moreover, Phoenicia, like Israel, was now free to build its power; and Hiram of Tyre began to advance the fortunes of his city and to enjoy profitable joint ventures with Solomon.

Now what about excavations related to Solomon's reign? As a result of the work of Nelson Glueck at Tell el-Khaleifeh (midway between Jordanian Aqabah and Israeli Eilat) in 1938–1940, it was popular to identify the site as Solomon's seaport of Ezion-geber. But recently the identification has been greatly doubted, if not abandoned, and the tendency is to locate Solomon's port on an island in the vicinity. There is no general agreement on the matter, however. Also, after Glueck's work in the area south of the Dead Sea, it became popular to assign the rather extensive remains of a copper industry there to the time of Solomon and to claim that this was a dimension of Solomon's glory not even hinted at in the Old Testament. Now, however, Rothenberg has shown that this industry was incorrectly dated. Instead, the Egyptians operated the mines there during the fourteenth to the twelfth centuries B.C., and Egyptian mining activity in the vicinity came to an end by 1150. The mines were not operated again until the Roman period.[18]

---

18 Beno Rothenberg, *Were These King Solomon's Mines?* (New York: Stein & Day, 1972), 206–7.

Positively, however, excavations at Gezer, Hazor, and Megiddo reveal extensive Solomonic construction. Well-constructed walls and gates with typical Solomonic design were excavated at each site. The gates had a tower on each side, behind which stood a row of three guard rooms. At Megiddo in the Solomonic level, there were two stable compounds capable of holding a total of 450 horses, correlating with the reference in 1 Kings 9:19 (cf. v. 15), that says that in his store, or garrison cities, he kept horses and chariots. Although there is some debate over the date of the stables at Megiddo, they were probably built in Solomon's day and reused in Ahab's days a century later.

Interesting confirmation of an architectural detail appeared in the Megiddo excavations. In 1 Kings 7:12 Solomon's house in Jerusalem is described as having "three rows of hewed stones, and a row of cedar beams." In the Solomonic level at Megiddo, whenever a third layer of stones of the houses had been preserved, the top of them had been burned black. When charred chunks of wood were salvaged, they proved on analysis to be cedar. Phoenician architecture in Solomon's time used this style of construction, and it must be remembered that Solomon and Hiram of Tyre carried on extensive commercial relationships.

Of course we cannot expect to find remains of Solomon's temple and palace because Nebuchadnezzar thoroughly gutted Jerusalem when he took the city in 586 B.C. Excavations do reflect the greatness of Solomon's reign in general, however; thus there is no reason to doubt the biblical account.

Although Solomon's reign was glorious in many respects, it was increasingly characterized by idolatry, brought on by his marriages to many pagan princesses for diplomatic reasons. As shrines for the use of these women multiplied and spirituality among Israelites slipped, God announced that as judgment for his people's sinning, Solomon's kingdom would be divided and only the tribe of Judah would remain loyal to his successors (1 Kings 11:1–13). The prediction came true when Jeroboam led the northern tribes of Israel in rebellion against Solomon's successor Rehoboam (1 Kings 12:16–14:31).

SARGON II AND THE FALL
OF THE NORTHERN KINGDOM OF ISRAEL

Clouds of doom hovered over Israel almost from the time of the death of Solomon (931 B.C.) and the division of the Hebrew Kingdom into Israel in the north and Judah in the south. True, there were times of economic prosperity when Omri built Samaria, and Ahab constructed his "ivory" palace, and the kings enjoyed the income from the rich farming area of northern Palestine. But Jeroboam's idolatrous act of setting up the golden calves at Dan and Bethel as well as Ahab's introduction of Baal worship could only eventually incur God's wrath. Moreover, Scripture says that all of the kings of Israel walked in the steps of Jeroboam, and certainly their subjects shared in their evil practices. In punishment, God determined to use Assyria "the rod of my anger" (Isaiah 10:5 NKJV) to destroy Israel.

Assyrian contact with Israel began in 853 B.C., when Shalmaneser III fought a confederacy of Syrian and Palestinian kings allied against him at Qarqar (or Karkar) in Syria. At that time, ten thousand of Ahab's troops and two thousand of his chariots met defeat, as the Monolith Inscription of Shalmaneser (now in the British Museum) indicates. Following Ahab, Jehu of Israel paid tribute to Shalmaneser, a fact that is demonstrated by an inscription on the Black Obelisk of Shalmaneser (also in the British Museum). Between 782 and 745 B.C., Assyrian kings were mediocre, and their inactivity in the West gave courage to Judah, Israel, and surrounding nations. Then Assyrian power reasserted itself. Tiglath-pileser III (744–727) forced Menahem of Israel to pay tribute in 738 B.C.. And six years later, in response to the plea of Ahaz of Judah to protect him against Israel, the Assyrian swooped down on the northern kingdom, taking Gilead, Galilee, and Naphtali, and carrying their inhabitants to Assyria (2 Kings 15:29). This action is confirmed by Assyrian records.

Shalmaneser V succeeded Tiglath-pileser in 727 B.C.. Hoshea of Israel, along with other satellite nations, entertained ideas of revolt. Soon, however, the new king was on the job, and a three-year siege of Samaria began. At length, the Assyrians took the city, but the Bible indicates neither the name of the instigator of the siege nor the victor. Without doubt Shalmaneser V began the siege, probably in 725 B.C.; and he probably took the city in 723 B.C., just before the end of his reign. He did not live to complete the mopping up after the battle, however, and left that to his successor Sargon II (722–705 B.C.).

Sargon exploited the situation, claiming in his inscriptions credit for taking the city:

> I besieged and captured Samaria, carrying off 27,290 of the people who dwelt therein. 50 chariots I gathered from among them, I caused others to take their [the deported inhabitants'] portion, I set my officers over them and imposed upon them the tribute of the former king.[19]

Presumably the number of captives mentioned here came from the whole district of Samaria; it seems much too large a number for them all to have been housed within the walls of the city. Because Sargon took credit for the whole campaign and the victory, history books frequently name him as being responsible for the destruction of Samaria; apparently giving him credit for too much. Of course there is no debate about the fact of the fall of the northern kingdom of Israel. This account simply verifies from

---

19 Daniel D. Luckenbill, *Ancient Records of Assyria and Babylon*, 2 vols. (Westport, Conn.: Greenwood, 1968), 2:26.

Assyrian records what the Bible describes. Again archaeological discoveries attest to the accuracy of Scripture.

Presumably the number of captives mentioned here came from the whole district of Samaria; it seems much too large a number for them all to have been housed within the walls of the city. Because Sargon took credit for the whole campaign and the victory, history books frequently name him as being responsible for the destruction of Samaria; apparently giving him credit for too much. Of course there is no debate about the fact of the fall of the northern kingdom of Israel. This account simply verifies from Assyrian records what the Bible describes. Again archaeological discoveries attest to the accuracy of Scripture.

THE ATTACK OF SENNACHERIB

After the Assyrians took the northern kingdom of Israel and destroyed the capital city of Samaria, they began to pressure the southern kingdom, the kingdom of Judah. At length, in 701 B.C., the Assyrian king Sennacherib launched a full-scale invasion, taking much of the countryside and finally besieging the city of Jerusalem (*see* Isaiah 36–37; cf. 2 Kings 18:13–19:36). The good king Hezekiah of Judah was ruling at the time and Isaiah was the court prophet, serving at the right hand of the king to steady him in his hour of distress.

Fortunately for Hezekiah, Sennacherib overreached himself. As he taunted Hezekiah's defenders on the walls, he bragged about his conquests of numerous other peoples. Then he said, in effect, "Their gods could not save them and yours can't either." Such an allegation challenged God to act. The text says that just at the right time God intervened, apparently by bringing a plague on Sennacherib's army, and the Assyrian broke off the siege and went home.

Interesting confirmation of Sennacherib's involvement in this venture appears in two virtually identical inscriptions on clay cylinders found in his palace at Nineveh. One of these is in the British Museum in London and the other in the Oriental Institute Museum of the University of Chicago. Luckenbill translates:

> As for Hezekiah, the Jew, who did not submit to my yoke, 46 of his strong, walled cities, as well as the small cities in their neighborhood . . . I besieged and took. 200,150 people, great and small, male and female, horses, mules, asses, camels, cattle and sheep, without number, I brought away from them and counted as spoil. Himself, like a caged bird, I shut up in Jerusalem, his royal city. . . . As for Hezekiah, the terrifying splendor of my majesty overcame him . . . and his mercenary troops which he had brought in to strengthen Jerusalem, his royal city, deserted him.[20]

It is very revealing to see Sennacherib's attitude here. Obviously, something happened at Jerusalem to keep him from capturing the city; his statement implies that he did not take it. In an effort to cover up his defeat, he made the best of a bad situation and played up the successes he did have. Nowhere did he claim conquest of Jerusalem. On this same invasion of Judah, Sennacherib was successful in conquering Lachish and memorialized the fact by devoting a couple of walls of his palace in Nineveh to a pictorial representation of the siege and capture of the city (now on display in the British Museum). Conquest of Jerusalem and destruction of the Judean kingdom no doubt would have prompted a much more grandiose artistic celebration.

After Sennacherib's attack, God gave the kingdom of Judah another century of existence. During that time the Assyrian Empire fell and the Neo-Babylonian Empire rose from its ashes. Finally, the Babylonians under Nebuchadnezzar destroyed the kingdom of Judah, the city of Jerusa-

---

20 Ibid., 2:120–21.

lem, and the temple in 586 B.C., carrying large numbers of Hebrews into captivity.

CYRUS THE GREAT OF PERSIA
AND THE RETURN OF THE JEWS

The Old Testament is full of threats and warnings that God would send the Hebrews into captivity for their idolatry and their general unfaithfulness to him. It also predicted that God in mercy would restore the Jews to their homeland at the end of seventy years of captivity. True to that promise, God put it into the heart of Cyrus the Great of Persia to allow the Jews to go back home. The biblical account of Cyrus' decree appears in 2 Chronicles 36 and Ezra 1. Again the Bible reader might ask, "Is this just a nice pious statement of how God cares for His people?"

The historical situation behind the decree was this. First, Cyrus the Great of Persia conquered the Babylonian Empire in 539 B.C. Then, as a humane man and also a wise administrator who wanted to eliminate resentment against him, he permitted all the captive peoples who had been carried off by the Assyrians and Babylonians to return to their ancestral homes. Moreover, as a somewhat superstitious man and a good polytheist, he asked these peoples to pray to their gods for him. Finally, he had an especially important reason for resettling the Jews in Palestine.

The reason for his allowing the Jews to resettle was that he had plans to invade Egypt and to add that land to his empire, so he wanted a stable, friendly situation in Palestine, which would provide him with the corridor to Egypt. Presumably Cyrus issued separate decrees to each of the captive peoples about his permitting them to return home. The decree to the Jews appears in Ezra 1.

Cyrus' own statement about all this appears on the Cyrus Cylinder, which Hormuzd Rassam found in Babylon in 1879. Now in the British Museum in London, the cylinder is on display for all to see, as a further witness to the historicity of the Bible.[21]

HISTORICAL TRUSTWORTHINESS OF THE BIBLE

A treatment of these several Bible narratives has shown that at point after point modern scholarship has either demonstrated the accuracy of a biblical passage or event or at least has shown an account to be plausible. The skeptical reader may assert that in the situations described in this chapter the author has been a playing with the evidence. They may also claim that in other instances a case cannot be made for historical reliability. As a matter of fact, while historical and interpretive *problems* do exist, modern scholarship has not proven a single historical *error* in Scripture. These accounts have been chosen because they are fairly familiar or because they may be discussed in a reasonably brief and uncomplicated way.

---

21 For a translation, see James B. Pritchard, ed., *Ancient Near East, An Anthology of Texts and Pictures* (Princeton: Princeton University Press, 1958), 1, 206–8.

CAN I REALLY BELIEVE IN THE INSPIRATION OF SCRIPTURE?

The world has been built by inspired people. The inventive genius of Thomas A. Edison inspired him to develop the phonograph, the incandescent electric lamp, and the talking motion picture, along with more than one thousand patented inventions. Shakespeare produced inspired dramas that reflect poetic genius and insights into human nature and that have stood the test of time. Handel was inspired to write the magnificent and ever-popular *Messiah* in fewer than twenty-five days.

On lesser levels, inspired people are all around us. We sometimes say that inspiration makes the world go around. For example, there is the newspaper columnist who writes an inspired editorial that helps bring together contentious or warring factions in a community; there is a high-school student who is inspired by a science assignment to produce an experiment or project that wins an award at a science fair; or there is an athlete who draws inspiration from the challenge of the moment or supporters or a role model to win a gold medal at the Olympics.

Because our awareness of inspired people is a part of everyday life, we often do not have a very clear idea of what the inspiration of Scripture involves. In fact, when it comes to the inspiration of the Old Testament prophets, our perception of that individual is somewhat fanciful. The prophet often comes across as a wild-eyed figure who has rather ecstatic visions. Popular spirituals do little to clarify our thinking about the prophets. Certainly this is true of such examples as "Ezekiel Saw de Wheel, 'Way up in de Mid'l of de Air," (based on Ezekiel 1) and "Dry Bones," a parody on the resurrection of the body (based on Ezekiel 37). The truth of the matter is, however, that the prophets did not commonly receive ecstatic visions. Nor did they often even predict the future. Their primary function was to call their people to social and ethical responsibility, to weed out the social and ethical corruption they saw everywhere.

DEFINITION OF INSPIRATION

To *inspire* basically means "to breathe in," and inspired Scripture involves the claim that it is God-breathed. In fact, 2 Timothy 3:16 bluntly asserts in preferred translation, "All Scripture is God-breathed." If all Scripture is God-breathed, it is exactly what God wanted to say. If it is exactly what He wanted to say, nothing is lacking that He wished to include and nothing is added that He might wish left out. Moreover, the very words He wanted used are there, with all their intimations and innuendoes and implications. Above all, if Scripture is God-breathed, it is completely accurate; for God is the God of all truth and cannot commit error.

In saying that the very words are what God wanted used, we do not mean that He merely dictated to a penman. The fact that there is such a variety of style and vocabulary in the books of the Bible and that the personality of the writer shines through should be evidence enough that God did not destroy the individuality of the writers. Thus, the

Bible is a divine and a human book; divine truth is passed through the personality and experience of the authors of Scripture. Therefore, we may think of inspiration as a work of God in which He guided the writers of Scripture to pen the exact words He wished recorded. This guidance did not violate the personality of these writers, yet it guaranteed accuracy of doctrine, judgment, and historical and scientific fact.

This God-breathed view of inspiration is the only one that takes into account all the claims of the numerous biblical references on the subject. We must reject all other theories of inspiration as inadequate. For instance, it is not enough to say that writers of Scripture possessed some special genius or insight, such as that demonstrated by a Milton or a Bunyan or a Shakespeare. Too much that appears in Scripture is infinitely beyond the comprehension or imagination of the most brilliant or even the most spiritual of men. Nor is it sufficient to say that inspiration is partial—applying only to truths unknowable by human reason and not to historical sections of the Bible. How can we trust the Bible if portions are shot through with error; how can we know if the doctrinal sections are reliable? Neither can we be satisfied that inspiration is merely conceptual—extending to the ideas, but not to the words. Ill-chosen words may mute the force of a concept, change the nature of its impact, or alter the whole direction of its argument. We cannot settle for less than some sort of control over the very words of Scripture and the guarantee of their accuracy.

A definition of inspiration often quoted in books that take a high view of inspiration is that of Professor Louis Gaussen of Geneva (about 1850): "[Inspiration is] that inexplicable power which the Divine Spirit put forth of old on the authors of holy Scripture, in order to their guidance even in the employment of the words they used, and to preserve them alike from all error and from all omission."[1]

Briefly analyzed, this definition says that inspiration is *inexplicable*, we cannot tell exactly how God did it; the *Divine Spirit*, the third person of the Trinity, is the agent; *of old* indicates there is no such inspiration now, which limits the time of inspiration; *authors of holy Scripture*, confines inspiration to writers of the Bible; *in order to their guidance* indicates purpose and method (the Holy Spirit sometimes guided them to use personal observation, oral information, written sources, or direct revelation); *employment of words* means that inspiration extends to the choice of words used; *from all omission*, the Bible is complete, we do not expect to find a seventh chapter of Galatians or a twenty-ninth chapter of Acts.

DEFENSE OF INSPIRATION

It is all very well to insist on a high view of inspiration of Scripture. But it is now time to ask how modern thinkers with a naturalistic bent can be expected to believe that God actually did tell human beings explicitly what He wanted them to know.

Inspiration of the Old Testament

Biblical Claims to Inspiration

To begin with, in the Old Testament inspiration is everywhere assumed and even asserted. Early in Old Testament times, when there was no Bible, it is said that God spoke directly to individuals. And when they wrote down those words, they claimed that they were recording the message God had communicated. Moses, especially, was God's penman. For example, as the Israelites camped at the foot of Mount Sinai, God called him up into the mountain and said, "Thus you shall say to the house of Jacob, and

---

1 Louis Gaussen, *Theopneustia: The Plenary Inspiration of the Holy Scriptures,* trans. David Scott (Chicago: Moody, n. d.), 34.

tell the sons of Israel" (Exodus 19:3 NASB). Then he spelled out the content of that message, "Now then, if you will indeed obey My voice and keep My covenant, then you shall be My own possession among all the peoples . . . These are the words that you shall speak to the sons of Israel" (Exodus 19:5–6 NASB). Moses did as he was told and called the elders of Israel, and they and all the people responded, "All that the LORD has spoken we will do" (Exodus 19:8 NASB).

Subsequently, all the people participated in a sanctification process, introducing another element of this communication process. Not only did spokesmen claim to be uttering God's words, but recipients accepted and recognized them as such. This pattern continues throughout the rest of the Old Testament: God's spokesmen speak and their hearers recognize their words as God's binding message. Following the scene in Exodus 19 comes the recording of the Ten Commandments and numerous ordinances (Exodus 20–23)—God's words to them. Ultimately it could be said: "And Moses wrote all the words of the LORD" (Exodus 24:4; cf. Deuteronomy 27:8 NKJV). Moses was so sure that he was communicating God's specific word to His people that he declared in Deuteronomy 4:2: "You shall not add to the word which I am commanding you, nor take away from it, that you may keep the commandments of the LORD your God which I command you" (NASB).

Of course Moses is not the only Old Testament writer who wrote the words of God. Isaiah (Isaiah 30:8) and Jeremiah (Jeremiah 30:2) were commanded to do the same. Jeremiah claimed: "Then the LORD put forth his hand, and touched my mouth. And the LORD said unto me, Behold I have put my words in thy mouth" (Jeremiah 1:9 KJV). And David asserted: "The Spirit of the LORD spake by me, and his word was in my tongue" (2 Samuel 23:2 KJV). In fact, such expressions as "The LORD said," "The LORD spoke," and "The word of the LORD came" are sprinkled liberally throughout the Old Testament, a commonly quoted tabulation is that they occur 3,808 times in the Old Testament. The writers were convinced that they were minutely communicating the word of God.

Accreditation of the Messenger

Of course it is not enough that individuals should claim to be God's spokesmen. They needed to be accredited messengers. Moses was worried about that when God commissioned him to lead the Israelites out of Egypt. To assure Moses and the Israelites, He gave Moses a rod with supernatural powers. It became a serpent (Exodus 4:3), it initiated the Ten Plagues (e. g., Exodus 7:17), it helped give victory in battle (Exodus 17:9–13). Ultimately, Moses' leadership and message were accredited by a whole series of miracles—including the Ten Plagues, the crossing of the Red Sea, and a cloud that led the Israelites through the Sinai wilderness by day and a pillar of fire that led them by night. Especially, in connection with the giving of the Law, God sent supernatural phenomena that confirmed divine communication (Exodus 19:18; 20:18).

In numerous other ways and on numerous other occasions God let it be known that His messenger was a bona fide communicator of spiritual truth. For example, He enabled Elijah to perform seven miracles and Elisha fourteen. Isaiah's prophecy (Isaiah 37–38) of the destruction of the Assyrian hosts besieging Jerusalem in 701 B.C. came true and is confirmed by archaeological discovery. Daniel was able to accurately describe and interpret Nebuchadnezzar's forgotten dream and was publicly rewarded for it (Daniel 2). Later his miraculous deliverance from lions' den further demonstrated God's hand upon him (Daniel 6).

Human Acceptance and Recognition

The production of an inspired and authoritative Scripture follows a logical pattern. Writers claimed to speak for

God and to utter the very words of God. Then God accredited His messengers, making it clear that they were indeed His spokesmen with His message. Human acceptance and recognition logically followed. As noted above, the people of Israel believed that God was speaking to them through Moses and committed themselves to obey His dictates (Exodus 19:8). Subsequently the two tablets of the Law were placed in the ark of the covenant (Exodus 25:21), the most priceless possession of Israel; and all of Moses' laws (the first five books of the Old Testament, one fourth of the total) were written in a book (scroll) and kept beside the ark (Deuteronomy 31:24–26).

The commands of the Law were binding on Joshua, Moses' successor (Joshua 1:7–8); and they were enjoined on all the people of Israel in a great ceremony in the vicinity of Shechem soon after Joshua led them into the land (Joshua 8:30–35). Later, Jews who returned from the captivity fully recognized the Law of Moses as binding upon them (Ezra 3:1–2; Nehemiah 8:1–8; 10:28–29).

God promised Moses that He would raise up a whole line of prophets after him in Israel, culminating in the person and work of Jesus Christ (Deuteronomy 18:15–22). The primary function of these men was to proclaim the truth of God; and of course they would also predict the future. Joshua probably qualifies as a prophetic successor of Moses. The early Jewish work Ecclesiasticus (composed about 180 B.C.) calls Joshua the "successor of Moses in prophecies." His leadership in Israel was attested by miracles (crossing the Jordan and the fall of the walls of Jericho), and he did predict at least one event that came true (Joshua 6:26; cf. 1 Kings 16:34). In any case, Joshua 24:26 says that he "wrote these words in the Book of the Law of God" (NKJV), presumably referring to our book of Joshua. Since he wrote in the Book of the Law of God, it would appear that he simply added to the officially recognized writings of Moses.

Possibly Samuel the prophet wrote Judges and 1 Samuel to our designated chapter 25 and verse 1, and then he died. Presumably the prophets Nathan and Gad took up the account there (1 Chronicles 29:29), and the prophets Abijah and Iddo continued the narrative later (2 Chronicles 9:29). Other prophets apparently contributed to the writing of Kings and Chronicles. Actually the Hebrew Bible calls Joshua, Judges, Samuel, and Kings "the former prophets." Of course, writers of the many books of Old Testament prophecies were men who had official positions as prophets and whose messages were recognized as coming from God. We know less about the poetic books. David (a prophet according to Acts 2:30) wrote about half of the Psalms. Other writers of Psalms—Heman, Jeduthun, and Asaph—are also called prophets (1 Chronicles 25:1–5). Presumably Solomon wrote Proverbs, Song of Songs, and Ecclesiastes; and God spoke to him in visions and dreams like the other prophets.

While we do not have information on how all the Old Testament books were accepted by the Hebrews into their sacred collection (and there is a not space here to discuss what we surmise), we do know that by New Testament times the Hebrews recognized as Scripture only our present thirty-nine books. The order in which they placed them was somewhat different from ours, however. After the Law and the prophets, they listed a group of writings that began with the Psalms and ended with 2 Chronicles. Luke 24:44 seems to refer to the entire Old Testament in this arrangement when it speaks of law, prophets, and psalms (which headed the last section of the Hebrew Bible).

Witness of Archaeological and Historical Study

If Scripture is God-breathed, it should be minutely accurate. The modern mind finds it impossible to accept the inspiration of Scripture if it is shot through with historical error. As noted in chapter 1, archaeological and historical study have confirmed the accuracy of the narratives of the Bible at point after point, or at least have shown them to be plausible. There is no need to restate that evidence.

Rather it is useful to note other categories of support for the historical accuracy of Scripture. The Hebrew Scriptures mention some thirty or more foreign kings whose names have been found on documents contemporary with those kings. The list includes kings of Egypt, Assyria, Persia, Syria, Phoenicia, and Moab. At the minimum, discoveries show that these were historical persons; sometimes these documents connect the kings with the biblical narrative. In addition, about a dozen kings of Israel and Judah appear in the Assyrian records. Remarkably, all of these biblical kings appear in proper chronological order and relationship to known secular history.

The relative date of Shishak, king of Egypt, corresponds to that of Rehoboam (1 Kings 14). The relative dates of the kings of Assyria and Egypt as cited on the monuments of their respective countries correspond with what we find in the Old Testament books. The relative dates of the Babylonian kings Nebuchadnezzar, Evil Merodach, and Belshazzar agree in both biblical and secular accounts. The analogous dates of the Cyrus of Ezra, the Darius of Haggai and Zechariah, and the Xerxes and Artaxerxes of Ezra are certainly correct.

The histories of the Sumerians, Assyrians, Babylonians, Persians, Egyptians, Hittites, Phoenicians, Philistines, and others have emerged from the shadows and in most instances have come into the full light of knowledge and understanding. What is said in Scripture about all these nations rings true in either a specific or, at least, a more general way.

Dozens of Old Testament cities have been excavated, providing either confirmation of the biblical narrative or at least shedding light on what life was like in biblical times. Ur, Babylon, Nineveh, Samaria, Jerusalem, Dan, Jericho,

Tirzah, Lachish, Dothan, Tyre, Susa, Memphis, and Thebes are some of the interesting sites that appear on the expanding list.

The Witness of Textual Preservation

By now the reader may be thinking, "What if I do accept the idea that the Old Testament is inspired? So many centuries have gone by since the books were written that the originals have been compromised by copyists' errors. Look at how many errors or variations have crept into works of Plato or Aristotle or Shakespeare."

As a matter of fact, the ancient Hebrews virtually worshiped the text of the Old Testament. Knowledge of their high regard for it should help modern believers respect it more highly as well as to accept its inspiration. The Hebrew scribes, or Sopherim, between about 400 B.C. and A.D. 200, tried to establish and maintain the true text of the Old Testament. In connection with this effort they made a practice of counting the verses, words, and letters of each Bible book and of appending this information in order to give future copyists a standard against which to check the accuracy of their copies.

The traditional Hebrew text achieved its standard form early in the second century A.D. The form was based on and substantially agreed with a much earlier textual tradition, as the Dead Sea Scrolls demonstrate. But the text of the scribes or custodians of the Bible was still only consonantal; it had no vowels or accent marks.

The work of Masoretes picked up where that of the Sopherim left off. Called Masoretes because they preserved in writing the oral traditions (Masora) concerning the biblical text, these Jewish scholars lived primarily in Tiberias on the western shore of the Sea of Galilee during the period A.D. 500 to 950. Most prominent among them were the learned Moses ben Asher and his son Aaron. The present Hebrew Bible is based on a ben Asher text.

The Masoretes sought not only to determine the exact text handed down to them but also to pass it on to future generations without change. To protect against copyists' errors and alterations, they filled the side margins with all sorts of data concerning how often and where various words and phrases appearing in a given line of the text could be found elsewhere.

The special contribution of the Masoretes was to provide the text with vowels and accent marks. This they achieved with a system of dots and strokes. Their task was not to invent pronunciations but to pass on received or accepted pronunciations and to decide between debatable ones. And of course the issue for them was not merely correct pronunciation, because a slight change in vowel pointing or pronunciation would, for instance, could turn a noun into a participle.

As the Masoretes strove to provide vowels and to protect the true text, they had to engage in a certain amount of textual criticism. But their reverence for the text would not permit them to make changes in it, so they worked out an ingenious system of editorial notes. Where it appeared to them that a copyist's error had occurred, they left the error written in the text (a *kethib* wording—that which is written) but put vowel markings with it for a preferred wording (*qere*—that which is to be read) and inserted the consonants for that reading in the margin. They also indicated a limited number of words that probably should be omitted altogether. The meticulous efforts of the Masoretes and the Sopherim before them has resulted in a marvelously successful preservation of the Old Testament text. What the Masoretes passed on to later centuries was extremely carefully copied by hand until the advent of the printing press. So, it may be confidently asserted that of all ancient Near Eastern literature, the Old Testament is unique in the degree of its preserved accuracy.

Information concerning the accuracy of the Old Testament text led the eminent Robert Dick Wilson, formerly of Princeton, to conclude:

> An examination of the Hebrew manuscripts now in existence shows that in the whole Old Testament there are scarcely any variants supported by more than one manuscript out of 200 to 400, in which each book is found. . . . The Massorites have left to us the variants which they gathered and we find that they amount altogether to about 1,200, less than one for each page of the printed Hebrew Bible [2].

Moreover, as William Henry Green, also formerly of Princeton, has shown, "The various readings are for the most part of a trivial character, not materially affecting the sense."[3]

Until World War II, the oldest Hebrew manuscript of any length did not date earlier than the end of the ninth century, and the oldest complete Hebrew Bible is dated about a century later. Then, in the spring of 1948, the religious and academic worlds were rocked with the announcement that an ancient Isaiah manuscript had been found in a cave at the northwest corner of the Dead Sea in an area called Qumran. Since then a total of eleven caves around Qumran have disgorged their treasures of scrolls or fragments. In addition, portions of biblical scrolls have been found in other caves in the region of the Dead Sea and in excavations at Masada. Tens of thousands of fragments have been recovered. While most of the materials are nonbiblical, several hundred fragments bear Scripture portions. So far, all Old Testament books except Esther are represented in

---

2 Robert D. Wilson, *Scientific Investigation of the Old Testament,* with revisions by Edward J. Young (Chicago: Moody, 1959), 69–70.

3 William Henry Green, *General Introduction to the Old Testament:The Text* (New York: Scribner, 1898), 179.

the finds. As might be expected, fragments of Old Testament books quoted most in the New Testament (Deuteronomy, Isaiah, and Psalms) are the most numerous. The longest and most intact biblical scrolls include two of Isaiah, one of Psalms, and one of Leviticus.

The significance of the Dead Sea Scrolls is tremendous. First, they have pushed the history of the Old Testament text back a thousand years (which dates them during the first two centuries B.C. and the first century A.D.). Second, they have provided an abundance of critical material for research on the Old Testament, comparable to what has been available to New Testament scholars for many years. Third, they have helped establish the accuracy of the Old Testament text.

As an example of the last point, the complete Isaiah manuscript from Qumran (commonly identified as I Q Is[a]) became available to the scholarly world at the time when the Revised Standard Version translation committee was preparing its new version. The RSV committee decided to adopt thirteen readings for their translation, based on the new manuscript. Millar Burrows, a member of the translation committee, later concluded that some of these readings were unwarranted, and in five of the thirteen instances, the Masoretic reading should have been retained.[4] Burrows observed further, "It is a matter for wonder that through something like a thousand years the text underwent so little alteration. As I said in my first article on the scroll, 'Herein lies its chief importance, supporting the fidelity of the Masoretic tradition' "[5]

The Witness of Jesus

The testimony of Jesus Christ is another powerful confirmation of the inspiration of the Old Testament. One of

---

4 Millar Burrows, *The Dead Sea Scrolls* (New York: Viking, 1955), 305.
5 Ibid., 304.

His most direct statements appears in Matthew 5:17–18: "Do not think that I came to abolish the Law or the Prophets. I did not come to abolish, but to fulfill. For truly, I say to you, until heaven and earth pass away, not the smallest letter or stroke shall pass away from the Law, until all is accomplished." (NASB). In the larger context of Matthew 5, it is clear that He was claiming the Old Testament to be of divine origin, binding on the Jews to whom He was speaking.

Apparently He was using *the law* here to stand for the whole Old Testament. In Matthew 5:17 He mentioned *law and prophets* but in verse 18 presumably found it unnecessary to repeat *prophets*. Elsewhere He used *law* to refer to passages outside the first five books of the Old Testament (called the Law or Torah). See, for instance, John 10:34 where He quotes Psalm 82:6. The Matthew 5:17–18 reference is especially significant because it appears in the Sermon on the Mount, which even the more severe textual critics certainly acknowledge as a true statement of Jesus Christ.

This passage is not an isolated indication of Jesus' witness, however, because He always supported the full truthfulness of Scripture in His parables, miracles, and comments on them, as well as in His numerous conversations. Hundreds of New Testament passages attest the fact. On occasion He spoke directly of divine inspiration of individual portions of the Old Testament, as for instance in Mark 12:36, where He referred to Psalm 110:1. Three times during His great-temptation experience, He appealed to the authority of the Old Testament to rout the Tempter (Matthew 4:4, 7, 10). And He very pointedly remarked that "Scripture cannot be broken" (John 10:35 NKJV); that is, it cannot be annulled or abrogated. Even Jesus' enemies among the Pharisees and Sadducees never accused Him of disrespect toward or questioning of their sacred Scriptures.

The New Testament Witness

Jesus' testimony to divine inspiration of the Old Testament is corroborated and supplemented throughout the rest of the New Testament. Paul, as a good Pharisee, would be expected to support the accuracy and validity of the Old Testament at all times. The writer to the Hebrews likewise subscribed to God's involvement in the process of revelation and inspiration: "In the past God spoke to our forefathers through the prophets at many times and in various ways, but in these last days he has spoken to us by his Son" (Hebrews 1:1–2 NIV). One of the most significant New Testament passages on Old Testament inspiration is 2 Peter 1:20–21, "Above all, you must understand that no prophecy of Scripture came about by the prophet's own interpretation. For prophecy never had its origin in the will of man, but men spoke from God as they were carried along by the Holy Spirit" (NIV). The clear teaching of this passage is that the revelation of God did not come when great religious leaders of the past sought to make some religious pronouncement, but when certain holy men, chosen instruments, spoke as they were moved by the Holy Spirit.

The Witness in Judaism

What the Old Testament claimed for itself in terms of inspiration and what Jesus and the New Testament writers supported in this regard was further attested to in Judaism. The very high regard that Jews had for the Old Testament, is evident from many passages in the Talmud (an encyclopedia of Jewish tradition), but it is especially spelled out in the forthright statement of the first century historian Flavius Josephus:

> How firmly we have given credit to these books of our own nation is evident by what we do; for during so many ages as have already passed no one hath been so bold either to add anything to them, to take anything from

them, or to make any change; but it is become natural to all Jews, immediately and from their very birth, to esteem these books to contain divine doctrines, and to persist in them, and if occasion be, willingly to die for them.[6]

The Witness of Fulfilled Prophecy

Much of the argument defending the above-presented inspiration of Scripture is based on an internal defense, arising from Scripture itself. Fulfilled prophecy also marshals testimony from the events of history. But before looking at specifics, it is important to consider the nature and purpose of both the prophet and biblical prophecy.

A true picture of the biblical prophet depicts him in his primary function of a forthteller—a social and political reformer, a preacher of righteousness, a religious revivalist, a predictor of judgment or blessing who announced the will of God and called for complete obedience to Him. As a monitor of God's people, he denounced prevailing sins, threatened the people with the terrors of divine judgment, warned them of approaching danger, and called them to repentance. He also brought a message of consolation and pardon.

But he was also a *foreteller*, a predictor of the future. This foretelling did not constitute an appeal to idle curiosity but rose as a result of the conditions of that time, being inseparably connected with the religious and spiritual message that the prophet was called to proclaim to his own generation. For example, a prediction of great blessing awaiting God's people in the future clearly indicated that they would survive their immediate troubles and that they should be encouraged. Further, the prophet dealt with existing sinfulness by predicting minutely the first coming of Christ and His redemptive work.

---

6   Josephus, *Contra Apionem* 1.8.

Predictive prophecy is a manifestation of God's power and glorifies His Person, exalts His redemptive work in Christ, demonstrates his love and concern for human beings lost in sin, and sets forth the divine character of His revealed Word. God Himself speaks to the apologetic value of fulfilled prophecy. A particularly pointed passage is Deuteronomy 18:18–22. There God tells Moses that He will raise up prophets, put His words in their mouths, and the people will know whether the prophet is speaking God's word by noting whether his predictions were true ("if the word does not come to pass or come true, that is a word which the LORD has not spoken," v. 22 RSV). An excellent supporting statement appears in Isaiah 41:21–23, where the test of the false gods is whether they can "declare to us the things to come" (v. 22 NKJV). Only an omniscient (all-knowing) and omnipotent (all-powerful) Being knows the future and can order events to cause them to happen.

It is clear that God Himself puts great stock in fulfilled prophecy and attaches great significance to it. The book of Matthew, especially, records events in the life of Christ that occurred in fulfillment of prophecy ("that it might be fulfilled" is a recurring refrain): (1) the virgin birth (Matthew 1:22–23; cf. Isaiah 7:14); (2) the flight into Egypt (Matthew 2:15; cf. Hosea 11:1); (3) Herod's slaughter of the infants in Bethlehem (Matthew 2:16–17; cf. Jeremiah 31:15); (4) the triumphal entry into Jerusalem (Matthew 21:4; cf. Zechariah 9:9); (5) the purchase of the potter's field with Judas' betrayal money (Matthew 27:4–10; cf. Jeremiah 18:1–4; 19:1–3; Zechariah 11:12–13); and (6) casting lots for Jesus' garments at the time of the Crucifixion (Matthew 27:35; John 19:24; cf. Psalm 22:18). This attention to recording fulfilled prophecy also appears in Mark, Luke, John, Acts, and James.

Predictive prophecy is a declaration of future events that lies beyond the ability of human wisdom to forecast. Such prediction is rooted in the omniscience of God and thus prophecy must be divine revelation. Prophecy must also be more than a good guess or conjecture. It must contain sufficient specifics that can be verified by means of its fulfillment. It must not be confused with the prediction of trends in business or politics, the outcomes of which are not necessarily certain or accurate. Nor must it be confused with scientific predictions, which are judgments based on a confidence in the continued orderly routine of nature.

Rather, prophecy involves statements about the future acts of individuals and society that are, from a human standpoint, unpredictable or unknowable. True prophecy is peculiar to the Bible and pervades it, is often minute in its particulars, and frequently deals with a very remote time. Often Bible students who deny the supernatural try to date the statements of the prophets very late to make them appear to be historical rather than predictive statements. But it is not always possible to date the Old Testament prophecies late enough to make them out to be historical statements, and biblical critics have given up trying to make them all appear to be historical.

Some Concrete Examples of Fulfilled Prophecy

ANCIENT EGYPT

A study of the fulfillment of Old Testament prophecy would fill at least one book, but a few examples of how fulfillment supports biblical inspiration can be briefly described. The two great cities of ancient Egypt were Memphis and Thebes. Both appear only in the prophetic writings of the Old Testament. Memphis is called Noph in Isaiah 19:13; Jeremiah 2:16; 44:1; 46:14, 19; Ezekiel 30:13, 16; and called Memphis in Hosea 9:3, 6. Hosea predicted that, with the destruction of Israel, many Jews would settle in Egypt, especially at Memphis; Jeremiah (44:1) describes the fulfillment of the prophecy. Ezekiel also predicted the destruction of the city's idols and images (Ezekiel 30:13, 16), and Jeremiah foretold the utter destruction of the city (Jeremiah 46:14, 19). Both of these prophecies have been completely fulfilled.

One would hardly have expected the destruction of the great old city of Memphis (capital of Egypt for about a thousand years, during the Old and Middle Kingdom periods), which was the largest city in Egypt in the days of the prophets just noted. The beginning of the fulfillment came when the Persian, Cambyses I, took the city in 525 B.C. Further decline occurred with the conquest of Alexander the Great in 332 B.C. and the construction of the rival city of Alexandria. By the time of Christ, Alexandria had replaced Memphis as the largest city in Egypt. The Christian Roman emperor, Theodosius (A.D. 379–95), in his campaign against paganism, ordered the destruction of the temples of Memphis and the desecration its statues. Then in A.D. 638, when the Arab Muslims conquered the area, they decided to move the capital to the newly founded city of Cairo, some fifteen miles to the northeast. Memphis became a so-called quarry for the new Muslim city. Not only did the Muslims gradually cart away the remains of Memphis, but, as strict monotheists, they, like Theodosius, destroyed its idols.

Today the prophecies against Memphis have been completely fulfilled. One can hardly find the remains of the ancient city that stretched some fifteen miles along the Nile. There are a few remnants though. A friend of mine told me about a nose or a hand of one of the idols that stuck out of several buildings in Old Cairo. A fallen forty-foot statue of Ramses II, one of his sphinxes, a few column bases and other minor ruins may be seen at a tourist stop alongside the modern road. Nearby, to the north, are some remains of the great temple of Ptah. Archaeologists have also found traces of a fort, a military camp, a palace and two or three other temples. The site has been so thoroughly ransacked it is doubtful that much of the ancient city ever will be located. Moreover, recovery is especially complicated by the high water table of the area.

Like Memphis, Thebes appears only in the prophetic Scriptures of the Old Testament (Jeremiah 46:25; Ezekiel 30:14–16; Nahum 3:8 NASB). Like Memphis, it appears by a name other than the familiar name in Scripture. The Old Testament calls it No or No-amon. *No* means "city" and is the equivalent of the Egyptian *Waset* or Greek *Thebes*. *No-amon* means "city of Amon." Like Memphis, Thebes would suffer judgment with a loss of population, but it was not to be utterly destroyed as Memphis was. The prophecies against Thebes were especially fulfilled on four occasions: (1) when Ashurbanipal of Assyria captured it in 663 B.C.; (2) when Cambyses of Persia marched through in 525 B.C. on his way to Nubia; (3) in rebellions against Ptolemy V (203–181 B.C.) and Ptolemy X (108–88 B.C.); and (4) when the Roman, Cornelius Gallus, punished it for revolting in 30 B.C. Unlike Memphis, Thebes has not utterly disappeared but has magnificent ruins. Roman Christian emperors and monotheistic Muslims seem to have concentrated attacks against ancient Egyptian polytheism on the population centers of northern Egypt, which they controlled more effectively than they did the south. Therefore Thebes (the capital during most of the Egyptian Empire period, c. 1570–1100 B.C.) did not suffer as many attacks on her idols and temples.

TYRE

The great ancient city of Tyre (c. sixty miles south of Beirut) was the target of Ezekiel's prophecies (26:3–12, 14, 19), during the time that the city was at the height of its power and glory. The prophet enunciated numerous specifics, but in general he predicted that Nebuchadnezzar of Babylon would attack the city, eventually break through her walls, take the city, and carry off much spoil. Then, without an indication of who would do it, or whether there was an interval, an attacker would throw the city's stones and timber in the water, with the result that the place where Tyre had stood would be as bare as the "top of a rock."

The year after Nebuchadnezzar's destruction of Jerusalem (586 B.C.), he swept into Phoenicia. Sidon capitulated, but Tyre put up a real fight. In fact, it withstood the Babylonians for thirteen years (585–572 B.C.), according to the Jewish historian Josephus.[7] Neither Josephus nor anyone else provides specifics of the surrender, but it must have involved the Babylonians' breaking through the walls, treading the streets, and taking much spoil, as Ezekiel had predicted. No other result could be expected after such a long siege. Fulfillment of the rest of the prophecy did not come for another 250 years.

At this point in our narrative, it is important to note that Tyre consisted of two parts— a mainland city and an island about a half mile offshore. The mainland city surrendered to Nebuchadnezzar, but the island city remained essentially independent because the Babylonians had no navy and Tyre was a great sea power. It is also possible that the island city had made some sort of agreement with Nebuchadnezzar in return for their continuing freedom. Nevertheless, in 332 B.C., Alexander the Great swept through Phoenicia. All the Phoenician city-states bowed to him except Tyre. Probably the Tyrians felt that their defenses, their off-shore location, and their fleet would save them. Undaunted, Alexander, without a fleet, decided to build a road out to the island city. For material, he used the rubble of mainland Tyre, which had remained unoccupied since Nebuchadnezzar's victory. In the process, he literally scraped the area bare like the top of a rock. The Tyrians fought heroically, trying to destroy the roadway as fast as Alexander built it. But finally, after seven months, Alexan-

---

7   Josephus, *Antiquities of the Jews*, X.11.1.

der won the struggle. Tyre was utterly destroyed. Many defenders died in the battle, and some were taken captive and sold into slavery; but many escaped on ships and went to live in Carthage or other friendly places.

In time, sands drifted against the roadway to the island city and a peninsula formed, jutting out from where the mainland city had stood. This peninsula is all the modern visitor to the area can see. Sometime later, Greek colonists came to live in the region, and there was a Greco-Roman Tyre there where Paul spent a week (Acts 21:3–4). But the later city had no connection with ancient Tyre historically or ethnically, and the prophecy may be declared completely fulfilled. The site of the ancient city is now an archaeological preserve. Modern Tyre stands a short distance away.

BABYLON

Babylon (fifty miles south of modern Baghdad) was one of the greatest cities of the ancient world, and it was the capital of one of the most powerful empires of the Near East during its brief period of dominance. The city itself had a double wall about eleven miles in circumference and at its height had a population of about a half million. Babylon came in for much attention in Scripture because it was guilty of destroying the kingdom of Judah, the city of Jerusalem, and the temple. Also, Babylon and Babylonian rulers figure in numerous biblical books, including Isaiah, Jeremiah, Ezekiel, Daniel, 2 Kings and 2 Chronicles.

Important and specific prophecies concerning Babylon appear in Isaiah 13:17–22; 45:1–3 and in Jeremiah 25:12–14; 50—51. These passages (some written even before Babylon had built her empire, c. 625 B.C.) make the following predictions: (1) Her enemies would be nations from the north, especially the Medes. (2) Cyrus, named centuries before his birth, would be the conqueror. As God's "anointed" (Isaiah 45:1), he would conquer the Babylonians at the end of the seventy-year captivity of the Jews in Babylon (Jeremiah 25:12). (3) Babylon would be as when God overthrew Sodom and Gomorrah, with her walls thrown down and so laid waste that she would furnish a home for wild beasts.

The beginning of the end came for Babylon with the death of Nebuchadnezzar in 561 B.C. His successors had little of the political and military genius that had characterized Nebuchadnezzar's forty-three-year reign. Their incompetence, coupled with the rise of the Medo-Persians, put Babylon in a precarious position. In fulfillment of prophecy, Cyrus the Persian rebelled against the Median royal family and established his line on the throne of the Median Empire. Subsequently, in October of 539 B.C., as God's anointed he defeated the Babylonians (who had taken Judah into captivity) and entered the city of Babylon. Bringing the captivity of the Jews to an end, he issued a decree permitting them to return to Palestine (see Ezra 1). A copy of the general decree permitting all captive peoples to return to their homes was found in Babylon and is on display in the Persian room of the British Museum.

The reduction of Babylon to the condition of Sodom and Gomorrah—a wasteland—took a long time. Cyrus did not need to fight against and ravage the city, so it remained intact after his conquest. Two rebellions against Persian rule during the reign of Xerxes (husband of Esther), 485–465 B.C., though, resulted in the destruction of some significant buildings. After that, there was continued decline until Alexander the Great triumphantly entered the city in 331 B.C. and sought to restore it; he did not live long enough to do so, however. The Roman emperor Septimius Severus reported that Babylon was deserted when he went there in A.D. 200. Although certainly the prophecy was fulfilled by Septimius' day, the archaeologist Austen H. Layard more specifically spoke to the condition of the site when he worked there in the last century. He called Babylon "a naked and hideous waste. Owls start from the scanty thickets, and the foul jackal skulks through the furrows. Truly 'the glory of kingdoms and the beauty of the Chaldees' excellency is as when God overthrew Sodom and Gomorrah. . . . "[8]

NINEVEH

Assyria earned the wrath of the prophets and the judgment of God for its treatment of the Hebrews. The Assyrians had destroyed the kingdom of Israel about 723 or 722 B.C. Subsequently, Sennacherib (704–681 B.C.) had attacked Judah in 701 B.C. and nearly brought the southern kingdom to its knees in the days of the good king Hezekiah and the prophet Isaiah (see Isaiah 36–37). Although Assyria had had other capitals, Sennacherib made Nineveh the great capital of the empire and it, especially, incurred the wrath of the prophets. Nahum specifically condemned the city: "Woe to the bloody city" (Isaiah 3:1); "Nineveh is laid waste" (v. 7); "the gates of thy land shall be set wide open unto thine enemies" (v. 13); "the sword shall cut thee off" (v. 15); "thy people is scattered upon the mountains" (v. 18). Zephaniah prophesied that God "will make Nineveh a desolation, and dry like a wilderness" (Zephaniah 2:13).

The great city of Nineveh, located 220 miles north of modern Baghdad on the east bank of the Tigris, was a populous city of some 170,000 at its height about 650 B.C. Its walls, about eight miles in length, still stand in places to a height of ten to twenty feet.

Assyria came unglued after the death of the great Ashurbanipal in 627 B.C. Within a year or so, Nabopolassar, father of Nebuchadnezzar, established Babylon's independence. By 614 B.C., both the Babylonians and the Medes were advancing into Assyrian territory. A couple of years

---

8 Austen H. Layard, *Discoveries among the Ruins of Nineveh and Babylon* (New York: Harper & Brothers, 1853), 413.

later, Scythians from the north joined the other two powers in a siege of the city. Nineveh fell in 612 B.C. in the surprisingly short period of three months, facilitated by the flooding of the Khosr River that ran through the city and swept away a section of the city's defenses. Nineveh was sacked and looted and the king died in the destruction. The attackers turned the city into a "ruin-mound and heaps of debris," and for three hundred years, according to archaeological evidence, the site was not occupied.

Nineveh was indeed "laid waste"; its gates were "set wide open"; the sword cut the people off and they were "scattered upon the mountains," where they regrouped and held out for another six years. Nineveh itself became a desolation. Dramatically, it passed out of existence immediately after its fall, instead of declining gradually, as did Babylon.

Inspiration of the New Testament

The inspiration of the New Testament stands or falls with that of the Old Testament, for claims of New Testament inspiration build on the assumption that the Old Testament is truly God's book. As noted above, Old Testament writers insisted in literally thousands of passages that they were uttering the words of God. The Old Testament was accepted as God's word by Jewry, by Christ, and by the early church. Its prophecies came to fulfillment as attested by history and the New Testament. Historical and archaeological studies have confirmed its historical accuracy at innumerable points.

Also, as noted above, ancient scribes treated the Old Testament as inspired and virtually worshiped the text as they laboriously and reverently copied it. As Jews scattered throughout the Gentile world during the period between the Old and New Testaments (c. 400 B.C. to the time of Christ), many of them could no longer speak Hebrew and read their Hebrew Bibles. In Greek-speaking Alexandria,

Egypt's Jews gradually translated their Bibles into Greek between about 250 and 150 B.C. This version, known as the Septuagint, was copied and read in the some 150 synagogues scattered across the Greek-speaking world by the time of Christ. Thus, Jews and Gentile "God-fearers," or proselytes, all around the Mediterranean lived with the concept of an inspired and authoritative book of God.

New Testament Claims to Inspiration

The New Testament goes on then to build on that concept or foundation of inspiration. The connection is clear from a passage like 2 Peter 3:2: "That you may be mindful of the words which were spoken before by the holy prophets, and *of the commandment of us*, the apostles of the Lord and Savior" (NKJV). Peter is obviously putting his own writings and those of the other apostles on the same level as those of the Old Testament and claiming the same authority for them. He extends the same recognition to Paul's writings: "Our beloved brother Paul, according to the wisdom given to him, has written to you, as also *in all his epistles*, speaking in them of these things, in which are some things hard to understand, which those who are untaught and unstable twist to their own destruction, as they do also the rest of the Scriptures" (2 Peter 3:15–16 NKJV). Jude claimed that "the words which were spoken before by the apostles of our Lord Jesus Christ" were absolutely reliable (v. 17 NKJV).

The apostle Paul on several occasions asserted that his words were divinely inspired and authoritative. For instance, he told the Corinthians, "the things that I write unto you are the commandments of the Lord" (1 Corinthians 14:37). He wrote to the Galatians that he had received his gospel by revelation from Christ (Galatians 1:11–12). He charged Timothy to "hold the pattern of sound words" which the younger preacher had heard from the apostle as if divinely uttered (2 Timothy 1:13, author's translation).

The apostle John warned against adding to or subtracting from the *words* of the book of Revelation under pain of being blotted out of the Book of Life (Revelation 22:18–19).

Accreditation of the Writers or Messengers of God

It is one thing for the New Testament writers or messengers of God to claim inspiration, it is another for them to be accredited to speak. In the first place, accreditation came from being associated with Christ as one of His apostles. Members of that apostolic circle presumably reported accurately what Jesus had said and done while he was on earth. And Jesus Himself had commissioned them to speak; an apostle is a "sent one" or a "commissioned one." Matthew, John, and Peter wrote as members of the Twelve. James and Jude were brothers of our Lord and also members of the apostolic circle. Mark wrote as an associate of, or understudy to, Peter. Paul was an apostle in the broader sense of one who had seen the risen Lord and had received a specific call to apostleship, thus being Christ's messenger or agent (Acts 9; cf. Romans 1:1; 1 Corinthians 1:1; 9:1–2; 15:8–10; Galatians 2:7–8). Luke wrote as Paul's close associate.

Second, accreditation also came from performing miracles. The apostles were associated with Jesus when he performed miracles. Then, on occasion, He sent them out to heal and cast out demons during His earthly ministry. After the Ascension, the apostles occasionally performed miracles on their own. For example, Peter and John healed the lame man at the temple (Acts 3); Philip performed miracles at Samaria (Acts 8:6–7); Paul and Barnabas worked miracles at Iconium in Asia Minor (Acts 14:3) and Paul performed miracles in Ephesus (Acts 19:11).

Third, accreditation came as the power of the Holy Spirit accompanied their ministry. This came especially in connection with Peter's preaching on the Day of Pentecost (Acts 2); the subsequent filling of the Spirit (Acts 4:31); the

Spirit's reception in Samaria (Acts 8:17); the Spirit's filling of Paul in Damascus (Acts 9:17); the Spirit's outpouring on Gentiles in Caesarea (Acts 10:44–46); and the Spirit's coming on Gentiles abroad (Acts 19:6). But the ministry of the Holy Spirit was evidently present on a regular and continuing basis as the apostles ministered during the first Christian century.

Human Acceptance and Recognition

As the apostolic company performed their ministries and wrote their gospels or epistles, their writings seem to have received almost immediate human acceptance and recognition. Some of Paul's epistles were probably the earliest written portions of the New Testament. Their recipients apparently accepted them immediately as inspired and authoritative. Paul, in one of his earliest epistles, had told the Thessalonians to see that "this letter be read to all the brethren" (1 Thessalonians 5:27). He told the Colossians to pass his letter to them on to the Laodicean church, and he also charged the Colossians to obtain a copy of the Laodicean letter (Colossians 4:16). As time went on, churches other than those to which the epistles were originally written sought copies of Paul's letters for their edification, accepted them as God's word, and understood that they were binding on them. In this fashion Paul's writings came to be collected and circulated as a group during the second century.

Meanwhile, the apostles, or persons closely associated with them, were writing the gospels, and these writings were finding acceptance in the early church. We read in early church literature that the "Memoirs of the Apostles" (the gospels) came to be read in church services alongside portions of the Old Testament as being God's Holy Word. The acceptance of Luke's gospel carried with it that of Acts. First John and 1 Peter enjoyed apostolic origin and therefore apostolic authority.

Some books, however, did not travel a smooth road to acceptance. Revelation, although written by John, had some difficult language; there was a question about the authorship of Hebrews but certainly not about the inspired nature of its contents; and questions arose over the authorship of 2 John, 3 John, 2 Peter, James, and Jude. Gradually uncertainties about the disputed books were overcome and they became universally accepted.

A local council meeting at Carthage in North Africa in A.D. 397 declared for the present twenty-seven books, with the proviso that no other books were to be used in the churches as authoritative Scripture. When the Sixth Council of Carthage (419) reaffirmed the earlier decision on the canon, it directed that the statement be sent to the Bishop of Rome and other bishops. From that time on there was little further debate on the subject of the New Testament canon in the West. The West's example and the influence of several great theologians in the East finally settled the matter there also. Since the fifth century there has been no serious controversy over the contents of the New Testament canon.

The Witness of Archaeology
and Historical Study to Inspiration

Late in the last century and early in the twentieth century, the spirit of rationalism or skepticism was especially strong in Western civilization. Critics doubted the Shakespearean authorship of Shakespeare, the Homeric authorship and historicity of Homer, and the traditional views of authorship and accuracy of Scripture. One of those who had a highly skeptical view of Luke's accuracy in his book of Acts was Sir William M. Ramsay (1851–1939), professor at Oxford and Aberdeen. Fortunately Ramsay was not content to live with his assumptions about the New Testament. He set out to investigate and especially led the way in exploring areas where New Testament events had occurred. Ultimately he became convinced of the absolute authenticity of Luke's account and wrote many books commenting on and defending the accuracy of the New Testament. His especially important works are The *Historical Geography of Asia Minor* (1890) and *St. Paul the Traveller and Roman Citizen* (1895). The best description of Ramsay and his work is W. Ward Gasque's *Sir William Ramsay: Archaeologist and New Testament Scholar* (1966). Numerous others have followed Ramsay (and some preceded him), minutely investigating biblical sites in Palestine, Syria, Asia Minor, Cyprus, Greece, and Italy—always with the same results.

Sometimes this research is specific, such as confirming the historicity of the name *Sapphira* (Acts 5:1) or discovering that the name *Candace* (Acts 8:27) was the name of a group of Ethiopian queens. (There is in the British Museum a large relief showing one of these queens whose name was Candace.) More often, though, such research simply throws light on the biblical narrative and shows what life was like at a biblical site in New Testament times. It is a different kind of apologetic, but no less effective, to stand in the marketplace of Philippi where Paul and Silas were attacked and beaten (Acts 16:19); to climb Mars Hill in Athens where Paul preached to the Areopagus Council (Acts 17:19); to pause before the judgment seat, or tribunal, where Paul appeared before Gallio in Corinth (Acts 18:12); or to sit in the great theater of Ephesus where the mob scene of Acts 19:29–41 took place. The New Testament has a greater ring of authenticity when we experience the reality of the New Testament narrative, courtesy of the extensive efforts of archaeologists. I have made it my business over the years of my professional career to visit and study every site mentioned in the New Testament in connection with the ministry of Jesus, Paul, and John. Under such circumstances, a sense of the reality of the New Testament narrative sets in and doubts flee away.

The Witness of Textual Preservation to Inspiration

It is often said that a little knowledge is a dangerous thing. That is certainly true when it comes to evaluating the text of the New Testament. Sometimes in the popular press or even in the university classroom the statement is made that in existing manuscripts of the New Testament there are many thousands of variations or errors. The inference or outright declaration is that it really does not matter what one's view of inspiration is. The manuscripts are so full of mistakes that they cannot be trusted. What is the layperson to do with such an assertion?

Fortunately, fuller knowledge leads to a far different conclusion. In the first place, the divergent readings often involve spelling, word order, and other such insignificant matters. Second, is the relative value of the manuscripts utilized in New Testament textual criticism. There are two classes of New Testament manuscripts: uncial and minuscule. The former are written in a kind of capital-letter script without ligatures and date from the third to the tenth centuries; there are 250 of them. The latter are written in lower case letters and in a cursive or freehand script; they total 2,646, according to the official listing, and date from the ninth to the fifteenth centuries.

As may well be suspected, the older, or uncial, manuscripts are more highly rated as reliable texts of Scripture. While there are more than twenty-six hundred minuscules of which we now know, most of them are of late date, and few play a very active part in the establishment of the correct text of the New Testament. This should heighten the realization that though many variant readings occur in New Testament manuscripts, most of them appear in late manuscripts considered to be of inferior value in determining a true text and are therefore not important. But we are still faced with a number of questionable readings, and Christians want assurance that they can depend on their

Bible. A word from Sir Frederic Kenyon, former director of the British Museum, is helpful at this point: "In the existence of various readings, therefore, there is nothing strange or disquieting. On the contrary, it is satisfactory to find that in spite of all these varieties of detail the substance of the record remains intact."[9]

Kenyon's statement may be supplemented by the assertion of the great New Testament authority, Dr. F. J. A. Hort, who held that only about one word in a thousand is under sufficient question to require the efforts of the textual critic to decide the correct reading.[10] When we realize that the Greek text that Westcott and Hort published is some five-hundred pages in length and that the words in question could therefore be put on a half page of it, our faith in the reliability of the New Testament is materially strengthened. But we may be helped still further by the statement of Bentley: "the real text of the sacred writings is competently exact, nor is one article of faith or moral precept either perverted or lost, choose as awkwardly as you will, choose the worst by design, out of the whole lump of readings."[11] Perhaps it would be well at this point to mention that the questioned readings referred to in these pages are not necessarily errors but rather problematic readings that require New Testament the efforts of scholars in order to solve the difficulty.

It is one thing to demonstrate that the New Testament text has been remarkably preserved from the fourth century to the present. It is quite another to deal with the assertion that the Gospels, for instance, gradually evolved

9   Sir Frederic Kenyon, *The Bible and Archaeology* (New York: Harper, 1940), 300.

10 C. F. Sitterly, "Text and Manuscripts of the New Testament," *The International Standard Bible Encyclopedia*, ed. James Orr, vol. 5 (Grand Rapids: Eerdmans, 1949), 2955.

11 Ibid.

into their present form during the early centuries of the Christian era and that Christ, who was originally considered to be a human being with a unique God-consciousness, in process of time became deified in the minds of the people by virtue of the increasing stories of His miraculous deeds. There was little objective information to hurl against liberalism of this kind during the last century, when its adherents were particularly numerous.

But thanks to the science of papyrology, which has developed so wonderfully during the last few decades, the picture is now very much changed. For the beginnings of this science we must credit B. P. Grenfell and A. S. Hunt, who excavated at Oxyrhynchus in the Fayum of Egypt from 1896 to 1906 and found literally tons of papyri. Written on a kind of paper made from the papyrus reed of Egypt, the unearthed documents covered a wide variety of topics—ranging from grocery lists and personal letters to copies of Homer and portions of Scripture. A number of languages were also represented, and the materials date to the first several centuries of the Christian era. It was possible to make such a find in Egypt because of the lack of rainfall and the preservative nature of the desert sands. Writings of like nature would have decomposed long before in other lands.

Since Grenfell's and Hunt's initial discoveries, other biblical and nonbiblical papyri have periodically come to light. At present, the number of papyrus fragments of Scripture stands at about seventy-six. The papyri manuscripts help to confirm the text found in the uncials and to bridge the gap between the original and the uncials.

Papyrology has had a phenomenal impact on biblical study. Since many of the papyri date to the first century, it is possible to establish the nature of that period's grammar and, on the basis of the argument from historical grammar, to date the composition of New Testament books. Says Millar Burrows,

Even in much later manuscripts, as we have seen, the type of Greek represented by the New Testament is that of the first century. Unless we resort to the wholly improbable hypothesis of a deliberate and remarkably successful use of archaic language, it is evident therefore that the books of the New Testament were written in the first century.[12]

Almost more important than the argument from historical grammar, however, was the publication of a papyrus fragment of the gospel of John (known as the Rylands Fragment) in 1935, variously dated by scholars between A.D. 120 and 140. If one allows time for the work to get into circulation, the date of the gospel is pushed back into the late first century. The other three gospels, the Synoptics, are always dated somewhat earlier. So archaeological discovery has brought us so near to the traditional dates of the writing of the Gospels that we are virtually breathing down the necks of the apostles. And since there was no sufficient lapse of time for legends to grow up around the person of Christ, as has been alleged, we may trust that the Gospel writers described Jesus as He was—the miracle-working Son of God. Kenyon concludes:

> The interval then between the dates of original composition and the earliest extant evidence becomes so small as to be in fact negligible, and the last foundation for any doubt that the Scriptures have come down to us substantially as they were written has now been removed. Both the *authenticity* and *general integrity* of the books of the New Testament may be regarded as finally established.[13]

---

12 Millar Burrows, *What Mean These Stones?* (New York: Meridian, 1957), 53–54.

13 Kenyon, *The Bible and Archaeology*, 288.

Parenthetically, the recent tendency of some scholars not in the evangelical tradition is to date New Testament books even earlier than traditional orthodoxy does. Albright concluded in 1955 that there was "no longer any solid basis for dating *any* book of the New Testament later than about A.D. 80.[14] Bishop John Robinson has rejected many of his earlier radical views and concluded in 1977 that the New Testament books were written between A.D. 47 and A.D. 70.[15]

It appears, then, that on the basis of the best current scholarship we may claim that the New Testament books were written during the first century and that the text has been marvelously preserved to the extent that what we have in our hands is essentially what was originally written. There are variations in the manuscripts, but most of them appear in inferior copies, and no doctrine or historical fact is put in jeopardy. The transmission of the New Testament text is so remarkable as to indicate a divine hand of protection and an argument for inspiration of the original.

The Witness of Internal Coherence

One of the most remarkable witnesses of the Bible to its inspiration is its coherence or unity of teaching. Consisting of sixty-six books; dealing with hundreds of subjects, written by some forty authors over a period of fifteen hundred years in Hebrew, Aramaic, and Greek; the Bible is remarkably unified in both theme and perspective. This is true in spite of the fact that the authors were kings, prophets, priests, fishermen, tax collectors, and others who lived and wrote in several countries of the Middle East and Mediterranean area.

---

14 William F. Albright, *Recent Discoveries in Bible Lands* (New York: Funk & Wagnalls, 1955), 136.

15 John A. T. Robinson, Can *We Trust the New Testament?* (Grand Rapids: Eerdmans, 1977), 63.

No one group or person put the Bible together. There was no collusion or construction of a master plan. Individuals simply wrote as they were "moved" (2 Peter 1:21), without knowledge of overall structure and most often without knowledge of what others had written or were writing. Books were collected as they were considered to be inspired, and *only in retrospect* was it discovered that the sixty-six books were one. Throughout, the Bible presents the same great doctrines concerning God, man, morality, salvation, and immortality. From the Fall in Genesis 3 as man capitulates to the temptation of Satan and sin enters the human experience to the defeat of Satan in Revelation 20, there is consistent treatment of the human problem. From the prediction in Genesis 3:15 of One who would deal with the sin problem, through the massive Messianic prediction throughout the rest of the Old Testament, to the ministry and crucifixion and resurrection of the Messiah in the Gospels, to His triumphant reign at the end times in the book of the Revelation, there is an amazing unity of focus on Jesus Christ. This incredible coherence, this incredible unity could not be contrived, could not rise from human engineering. It is evidence of divine origin. As Geisler and Nix observe, the "unity the book has must come from beyond them,"[16] i. e., the human authors.

The Witness of the Believer's Response

Now we return to the basic question of this chapter: Can I really believe in the inspiration of Scripture? We have made a case for the inspiration of the Bible. We have seen that the writers of both the Old and New Testaments claimed inspiration. God provided abundant accreditation of the writers of both testaments to demonstrate that they did indeed speak His words. There was immediate human

---

16 Norman L. Geisler and William E. Nix, *From God to Us* (Chicago: Moody Press, 1974), 57.

acceptance and recognition of the contents of both testaments. Archaeological and historical study has helped verify the accuracy and give a sense of reality to the text of both testaments. Then, too, the worshipful attitude that resulted in the text's meticulous preservation impresses us with a sense that God was present in the process as well as in the text. Further, fulfilled prophecy is a powerful argument for inspiration. In addition to the examples of fulfilled prophecy given in this chapter, we note the contribution of Canon Liddon, who is the authority for the statement that there are 332 distinct prophecies in the Old Testament that have been literally fulfilled in Christ.[17] The mathematical probability of all these being fulfilled in one man is so remote as to stagger the imagination. Finally, we found that internal coherence is a forceful argument for the inspiration of the Bible. Perhaps we are convinced. But there is another dimension to the argument of persuasion. When the Spirit of God speaks through the Word of God to the heart of the believer, communicating the love of God, forgiveness from sin, instruction for daily living, and divine peace in the midst of the turmoil of life, then the reader will really know that the Bible is inspired.

---

17 Floyd E. Hamilton, *The Basis of Christian Faith*, 3d rev. ed. (New York: Harper, 1946), 156.

Chapter 3

CAN I REALLY BELIEVE
IN MIRACLES?

When Roger Staubach led the Dallas Cowboys to two touchdowns in less than two minutes to win the 1972 NFC Championship over the San Francisco 49ers, the feat was called "the miracle victory." When a family of five walked away from a downed and demolished helicopter on the East coast of America with hardly a scratch early in 1994, the press called it a "miracle." In August of 1994 a series of tornadoes ripped through South Carolina. In one of the communities badly hit, the local sheriff said, "When you look out over the terrible devastation, the piles of bricks and twisted metal in places where buildings once stood, it is a miracle that no one was killed." As historians pump out books commemorating the fiftieth anniversary of World War II, the word "miracle" often appears. Gordon W. Prange called his book on the triumphant victory at Midway and the crushing defeat of Japan, *Miracle at Midway.*

In these and a host of other ways the word *miracle* occurs in popular jargon. And some, conditioned by such frequent repetition, will say, "Of course I believe in miracles," when a Christian asks them if they can accept a belief in the miraculous. The truth is, they do not really understand the question. Others, who believe in a philosophy of naturalism, hold that nature is supreme and nothing can interrupt its operation, not even God. As Albert Einstein said, " the idea of a Being who interferes with the sequence of events in the world is absolutely impossible."[1]

DEFINITION OF MIRACLE

Confronted by such opposing views and by the loose use of the word *miracle* we have to define what miracles are before we deal with the question of whether they are legitimate happenings in history. Probably the simplest definition, given by C. S. Lewis, is: "an interference with Nature by supernatural power."[2] But a definition by Machen is also helpful: "A miracle is an event in the external world that is wrought by the immediate power of God."[3] By this he means that a divine work is miraculous when God "uses no means but puts forth His creative power as He put it forth when He first made all things of nothing."[4]

Actually, Machen's definition has its limitations because, especially in Old Testament times, God apparently did use natural methods. For example, in opening a path for the Israelites through the Red Sea, He used intense wind (thus heightening natural phenomena) to lower the water level (see chapter 1). In blocking the Jordan for the Israelites to cross or in bringing about the fall of Jericho, He very possibly used an earthquake (see chapter 1). Of course in other instances, such as Jesus' turning water into wine or feeding the five thousand, God's creative power is evident.

1 Albert Einstein, "The Meeting Place of Science and Religion," in *Has Science Discovered God?* ed. Edward H. Cotton (New York: Crowell, 1931), 101.

2 C. S. Lewis, *Miracles* (New York: Macmillan, 1947), 15.

3 J. Gresham Machen, *The Christian View of Man* (New York: Macmillan, 1937), 117.

4 Ibid.

In other words, we may say that a miracle occurs when God steps in to do something beyond what could be accomplished according to the laws of nature as we understand them, as well as when God does something that actually may be in violation of the laws of nature. But we need to be careful here or we make our case too difficult. Although some miracles in the Old Testament or the New may violate a law of nature, they do not do so to such a degree that the laws of nature are thrown out of whack or large numbers of individuals are affected in various places. The only miracle that might have interfered with the functioning of the solar system was Joshua's "long day" (Joshua 10:12–14). And that is open to an alternate interpretation; i.e., the sun "was dumb" for a whole day and ceased to shine. So Joshua's long day becomes Joshua's long night, which could have been achieved by local atmospheric conditions; hence there was no need for the laws of the universe to be tampered with.

Moreover, miracles are beyond the powers of human beings and all of their intellectual or scientific ability. To be sure, God reveals His power or speaks in a general way at all times and to all the world through the laws or processes of nature (*see* Romans 1:20). But in miracles He speaks to particular individuals with a specific message to which He calls them to give heed.

THE PURPOSE OF MIRACLES

The average Bible reader, when confronted with the question of whether miracles could or did occur, may have the impression that miracles are scattered helter-skelter throughout the Bible. But they are not. They are not isolated events in the life of a remarkable person, whether Elijah, Daniel, or Jesus. They are related to a divine purpose. Actually, four periods in biblical history are especially characterized by them: the days of (1) Moses and Joshua, (2) Elijah and Elisha, (3) Daniel, and (4) Christ and the early church. In each case, miracles serve to accredit the message and the messenger of God at critical stages of the Hebrew-Christian tradition. In the days of Moses, God's servant needed to be accredited before his people and Pharaoh. The Israelites and Egyptians needed to know that God had sent Moses, and the message that he delivered was not his own concoction. Moreover, the miracles had to be of such a nature as to secure the release of the Israelites from Egypt and to carry them through the wilderness experience. Joshua, like Moses, also had to be accredited; and the Israelites needed to be settled in the land that God had given them. Because of powerful enemies, they required divine help to win battles and to occupy the land. Later, in the ninth century B.C., when apostasy in general and Baal worship in particular, threatened to exterminate the worship of God in the kingdom of Israel, miraculous works served to accredit the prophets, Elijah and Elisha, and to protect or perpetuate the orthodox faith. Then, in the days of the destruction of the temple and the captivity of the southern kingdom, the true faith was again in jeopardy of extinction. Under the circumstances, God interjected the miraculous.

During Jesus' ministry, He used miracles to demonstrate His deity, to prove that He was sent from God, to support His Messiahship, to lead His followers to saving faith, to give evidence of an inner spiritual rejuvenation (as in the case of the healing of the paralytic, Mark 2:10–11), and as an instructional aid to help prepare His disciples for the ministry they were to perform (e. g., Mark 8:16–21). And, of course, the miracles of the incarnation, the resurrection, and the ascension are essential to the divine provision of salvation for mankind. But, of course, the reason for the miracles was not only to accredit Jesus and His message; He sought to meet specific needs of individuals with His wonderful works. Miracles in the ministry of Christ are not to be thought of as the tricks of a magician or as entertainments to win the acclaim of the populace but as "deeds of mercy and love . . . . They are acts of divine grace to relieve human suffering, to dissipate doubt, and to prompt faith."[5] The same may be said of miracles in the days of Moses and Elijah and Elisha.

MIRACLES IN THE MINISTRY OF JESUS

To elucidate Jesus' miraculous ministry further, let us note that four Greek words appear in the Gospels to describe the supernatural works of Jesus: *teras* (wonder) speaks of their extraordinary character; *sēmeion* (sign) symbolizes heavenly truths and indicates Christ's immediate connection with a higher spiritual world; *dunamis* (power) describes an exercise of divine power and demonstrates the fact that higher forces have entered into and are working in this lower world of ours; *ergon* (work) refers to miraculous deeds that Christ came to do. The first three terms appear together in Acts 2:22, KJV: "Jesus of Nazareth, a man approved of God among you by miracles *[dunamesin]* and wonders *[terasin]*, and signs *[semeiois]*, which God did by him in the midst of you as you yourselves also know."[6]

Jesus Himself appealed to His miracles as His divine authentication.[7] In a discussion among leaders of the Jews and Jesus after He had healed the lame man at the Pool of Bethesda, the Jews accused Jesus of making Himself equal with God (John 5:18). He responded by saying that God the Father, John the Baptist, and the Scriptures bore witness to Him. Moreover, His works also bore witness: "the works

---

5 Bernard Ramm, *Protestant Christian Evidences* (Chicago: Moody Press, 1953), 132.

6 W. Graham Scroggie, *A Guide to the Gospels* (London: Pickering & Inglis, 1948), 203–4.

7 For discussion, see Ramm, *Protestant Christian Evidences*, 134–35.

which the Father has given me to finish—the very works that I do—bear witness of Me, that the Father has sent me" (John 5:36 NKJV). On another occasion some Jewish leaders asked Jesus to tell them directly whether He was the Messiah. He answered: "I told you, and you do not believe. The works that I do in My Father's name, they bear witness of Me" (John 10:25 NKJV). After John the Baptist had been thrown in prison, he sent two of his disciples to Jesus to ask whether He was the Messiah. Either John wanted to know for himself or he used this means to bring his disciples to full faith in Jesus. Jesus' reply was first to perform a number of miracles in their presence and then to say, "Go and tell John the things you have seen and heard: that the blind see, the lame walk, the lepers are cleansed, the deaf hear, the dead are raised, the poor have the gospel preached to them" (Luke 7:22 NKJV).

The miracles of Jesus were also designed to win His disciples. After His first miracle, turning water into wine at Cana, John observed: "This beginning of miracles did Jesus in Cana of Galilee, and manifested forth his glory; and his disciples believed on him" (John 2:11 KJV). And Jesus Himself in His discussion with the disciples about preparing a place in Heaven for them and about His identity said, "Believe Me for the sake of the works themselves" (John 14:11 NKJV).

Finally, remarkably, in dealing with a man sick of palsy, he said, "Your sins are forgiven you" (Matthew 9:2 NKJV); and "For which is easier, to say, 'Your sins are forgiven you,' or to say, 'Arise and walk'? But that you may know that the Son of Man has power on earth to forgive sins—then He said to the paralytic, 'Arise, take up your bed, and go to your house'" (vv. 5–6 NKJV). What Jesus was saying here was, "The power of working miracles demonstrated His authority in the spiritual domain.[8]

---

8 Ibid., 135.

Jesus' Miracles and the Literary Context

It is important to note that the miracles of Jesus Christ are an inextricable part of the gospel record. If they are cut out of the account, the record becomes unintelligible. Often events before the miracle set the stage for it and events after it are consequences that follow from it. For example, the raising of Lazarus in John 11 gave rise to a sequence of events that led to Jesus' death. Without the miracle, the Jews would not have been incited, and there would have been no crucifixion at that time. Again, the healing of the blind man in John 9 led to an agitation among the people and a series of actions on the part of the Pharisees, all of which would have been meaningless without the healing. So the efforts of antisupernaturalists to lop off the supernatural element from Jesus' ministry and to make Him merely a human Christ is doomed to failure from a literary standpoint.

Validity of the Witness to Jesus' Miracles

There are those who simply reject, out of hand, the witness of the New Testament to the miracles of Christ and the early church. But the courts of the world consider seriously the oral or written testimony of witnesses and accept it if they have no reason to doubt the integrity of the witnesses. Reasons for putting stock in the New Testament record are abundant.[9] First, most of the miracles were performed in public: along the road, in the temple complex, in a crowded house, during a synagogue service, in the presence of five-thousand men plus women and children (in the case of the feeding of the five thousand). Suspect miracles could have been contested on the spot. Second, some miracles were performed before unbelievers—not in the presence of supporters predisposed to accept the

---

9   For development, see Ramm, *Protestant Christian Evidences*, 140–44.

magical acts of their leader and to egg him on. Third, Jesus performed His miracles over an extended period of time, and they involved all facets of human experience: power over all kinds of disease, including death; control over nature (i.e., stilling the storm); creation (i.e., multiplication of a food supply, turning water into wine); supernatural powers of knowledge (i.e., He knew the thoughts of men); and more. His repertoire was not limited as was the repertoire of the impostors of history. Fourth, there are numerous cases in which those healed bore witness to their healing. Fifth, there is no record of early Christians', who buckled under persecution, exposing the miracles of Christ or the early church as fakes. Even Judas Iscariot, in his betrayal of the Master, did not do that.

Finally, as noted in chapter 2, it is no longer valid to claim that the New Testament books were written in the second century and later or embody an evolving tradition concerning Christ and the early church; i. e., to glorify the early human or humanistic element of Christ and the church by attaching magical or supernatural elements. All of the New Testament books must be dated in the first Christian century—in fact, most of them by shortly after the middle of the century. At least Matthew, Mark, Luke, and Acts were written while many contemporary witnesses (and subjects, as in the case of those whom Jesus or the disciples healed) were still alive and could either vouch for the miracles or expose Jesus and the disciples as impostors. There is no record of any of Jesus' enemies', during His lifetime or afterward, putting on a campaign to deny His miraculous powers. It seems that the best they could do was to charge that He was in league with the devil and that He worked His miracles by the power of Satan (Matthew 12).

Ramm is quite optimistic when he says: "The so-called Liberal interpretation of the Gospels in which a naturalistic Jesus could be separated from a theological Christ is now defunct."[10] As a matter of fact, the liberal press still pumps out books that try to discover the "historical Jesus," who was just a good person with a wonderful ethic, as recorded in the Sermon on the Mount (Matthew 5–7). And they charge that later the church added a dimension to the life and teachings of Christ that was not there earlier.

But we insist that the Gospels know nothing of a hiatus between the actual life and ministry of Jesus and the early church. If the gospel of Matthew is to be dated as early as A.D. 45 or 50, as even some liberals conclude, and if the books of Luke and Acts and nearly all of Paul's epistles date between A.D. 50 and 60, there is no time for such an evolutionary development. It is clear from the early chapters of Acts that the founding of the church occurred within days after Jesus' ascension. And the disciples and apostles continued the miraculous ministry that Jesus Himself performed (Hebrews 2:4) as a divine confirmation of their message and ministry. Moreover, the apostles (including Paul) adhered to the doctrinal line set by Jesus during His earthly ministry. And when it comes to salvation, the evangelical church, both in the early days and now, repeats more often than any other the admonition of Jesus to Nicodemus, "For God so loved the world that He gave His only begotten Son, that whoever believes in Him should not perish but have everlasting life" (John 3:16 NKJV). There is also no hiatus between Jesus and the early church on the one hand and the contemporary church on the other when it comes to basic theological development. Such a hiatus is imagined or contrived.

THE DENIAL OF THE SUPERNATURAL IN THE MODERN WORLD

But having said all this, we must acknowledge that there are a great many in the modern world who deny even

_____

10 Ramm, *Protestant Christian Evidences*, 154.

the possibility of miracles; thus, they operate within a frame of reference different from ancient and medieval persons. Up to the seventeenth century, people in the so-called Christian West lived within a supernatural frame of reference and accepted the possibility of miracles. But after the publication of Descartes' *Discourse on Method* (1637) and Newton's *Principia* (1687), the idea of a universe run by natural law and controlled by the force of gravity became the norm. And the tendency of a great many was to view nature as a closed system of causes and effects and to see the world as operating in a mechanical and determined fashion.

Two philosophers especially influenced modern thinking about miracles—Spinoza (1632–77) and Hume (1711–76). Spinoza in his *Tractatus*[11] took a pantheistic approach to miracles: God is identical with the universe, so there is no supernatural intrusion into nature from anything outside it. Moreover, nature follows a "fixed and immutable order" controlled by natural laws that cannot be violated. Therefore, miracles are impossible; whatever is reported in Scripture is, like everything else, subject to natural laws; thus miracle is eliminated.

Hume[12] constructed an argument against miracles that was more influential than was Spinoza's. Arguing empirically or from experience (what can be known from the five senses) and in the skeptical spirit of the eighteenth century, Hume came to believe that miracles were inconceivable. He held that the laws of nature had been established by human experience; and miracle is a violation of these laws. Since these laws are unalterably uniform, miracles

---

11 Benedict De Spinoza, "Tractatus Theologico-Politicus," in *The Chief Works of Benedict de Spinoza*, trans., R. H. M. Elwes (London: George Bell and Sons, 1883).

12 See David Hume, *An Inquiry Concerning Human Understanding,* ed. C. W. Hendel (New York: Bobbs-Merrill, 1955), Part 10.

cannot occur. Put more tactfully or less boldly, natural law describes regular occurrences; miracles are rare occurrences. Evidence for the regular is greater than that for the rare occurrences. A wise, rational individual will always opt for the greater evidence and should therefore never believe in miracles.

There has, of course, been a host of philosophers since Spinoza and Hume who have taken similar positions. Multitudes of men and women on the street subscribe to the naturalistic position that miracles either cannot occur or that the likelihood is so remote as to make the consideration of this possibility quite irrelevant. Of course, these views are based primarily on the concept that the natural universe is a closed system of cause and effect run by natural law.

Miracles and the Laws of Nature

But what are these so-called laws of nature? Do they preclude the possibility of miracles? As to the character of the laws of nature, Boettner observes:

> They are not themselves forces in nature, but are merely general statements of the way in which these forces act so far as we have been able to observe them. They are not powers which rule all nature and force obedience to themselves, but rather mere abstractions which have no concrete existence in the external world.[13]

In the same vein, C. S. Lewis concludes:

> We are in the habit of talking as if they caused events to happen; but they have never caused any event at all. . . . They produce no events: they state the pattern to

---

13 Loraine Boettner, *Studies in Theology* (Grand Rapids: Eerdmans, 1947), 61.

which every event—if only it can be induced to happen—must conform, just as the rules of arithmetic state the pattern to which all transactions with money must conform—if only you can get hold of any money.[14]

It should be clear, then, that the laws of nature are merely observations of uniformity or constancy in nature. They are not forces that initiate action. They describe the way nature behaves—when its course is not affected by a superior power. On the human plane, there is the constant introduction of new factors or forces to interfere with the normal (unhampered) course of nature. For example, chemicals mixed in certain quantities may produce a drug beneficial to human beings. If another force, such as heat or another chemical, is introduced, the result may be an explosion—or a deadly poison. Thus, human beings are constantly performing "miracles" as they interfere with nature. Thousands of their inventions violate the laws of nature. We know how to manipulate the laws of physics to fly huge heavier-than-air "buses" through the sky and to float and propel great steel ocean liners across the seven seas. Is God less than His creatures?

Lewis observes:

> The more certain we are of the law the more clearly we know that if new factors have been introduced the result will vary accordingly. What we do not know, as physicists, is whether supernatural power might be one of the new factors. . . . Miracle is, from the point of view of the scientist, a form of doctoring, tampering, (if you like) cheating. It introduces a new factor into the situation, namely supernatural force, which the scientist had not reckoned on.[15]

---

14 Lewis, *Miracles*, 71.
15 Lewis, *Miracles*, 70–71.

How Science and Religion Relate

Evangelicals reject the prejudice that one is scientist *or* Christian, that one is intellectual and naturalist or emotional and religious. Evangelicals believe in the uniformity of nature for all the practical purposes of science. They insist that emotion be verified by rational evidence; they believe that one may be a scientist and Christian. There need not be any basic conflict between science and religion. "Science . . . has for the most part now clearly seen that to seek to describe an order in nature does not imply the denial of a ground of nature." [16] Increasingly, there is a tendency to recognize that science is one thing and religion another. Science seeks to describe phenomena and to develop new inventions in the physical world. In short, it seeks to answer how. Religion seeks to describe phenomena and broaden horizons in the spiritual world. It seeks the reasons behind the phenomena. In short, it tries to answer why.

That this tension can be reconciled is clear from the fact that a number of outstanding scientists today are thoroughgoing supernaturalists—believers in miracles. The difficulty comes when human interpreters proceed on the hypothesis that miracles are impossible. Thus, a nontheistic worldview is made the criterion of history. Instead of examining the world to obtain a worldview, the unbelievers use their worldview to construct the history of the world. And the history they construct is self-contradictory.[17]

Moreover, the impossibility of miracles is predicated on a rather omniscient view of natural law. The assumption

---

16 C. J. Wright, *Miracle in History and in Modern Thought* (New York: Henry Holt & Co., 1930), 178.

17 Gordon H. Clark, "The Resurrection," *Christianity Today,* 15 April 15, 1957, 19.

is that experience is so extensive as to know how natural law *always* operates. As Geisler has observed, it is impossible on the one hand to know *"in advance* of looking at the evidence" that all experience is uniformly against the possibility of miracles or of a given miracle. On the other hand, one cannot claim that there are no miracles on the basis of "select experiences of *some,* persons" because others claim to have experienced them.[18] Furthermore, Geisler argues that if we subscribe to Hume's arguments against miracles, we should not believe in "any unusual or unique event from the past;" we would not admit "exceptions" to scientific "law" or "theory," and there would be no progress in science.[19]

More Openness to the Miraculous

Let us not be too antiquated in our defense of the miraculous. It is easy to set up straw men in our apologetic for the faith. For some time there has been a tendency to abandon the extreme position in the denial of miracles. At the turn of the century, Adolf Harnack, a great German liberal, could thus write, "Much that was formerly rejected has been reestablished on a close investigation, and in the light of comprehensive experience. Who in these days, for example, could make such short work of the miraculous cures in the Gospels as was the custom of scholars formerly?[20]

Since Harnack's day, Newtonian physics, with the advent of the quantum theory, has lost some of its grip. Without going into detail on the theory itself, we can simply note that its effect is to release people from some of the

---

18 Norman Geisler, *Miracles and Modern Thought* (Grand Rapids: Zondervan, 1982), 29.

19 Geisler, *Miracles and Modern Thought*, 31, 33.

20 Adolf Harnack, *Christians and History,*, 63, quoted in W. Sanday, *Outlines of the Life of Christ* (New York: Scribners, 1905), 101.

constraints of the mechanical concept of the world. Entities are not seen as being so totally determined as the Newtonian worldview had predicated. Indeterminism may occur in at least some small events, and that opens the door for some intellectual respectability of a movement toward a belief in miracles.

CAN I BELIEVE IN MIRACLES?

Can I believe in miracles? The answer is tied in with most of the other chapters of this book. Chapter 1 shows that in some instances the miraculous is plausible. Chapter 2 demonstrates that the biblical record as an inspired account purports to describe all sorts of miracles. Chapter 7 argues for the existence of God. If we accept His existence, then He presumably is not a limited God. If He is capable of creating the universe and humanity, then He is certainly able to perform other supernatural acts. If we can make a case for the resurrection of Christ (chapter 6), then we have established the fact or principle of miracle, and presumably others can easily follow. If we accept the deity of Christ (chapter 5) and the inspiration of Scripture, then there is no limit to His performing miracles. In the Bible we have a reliable record of His many miracles—thirty-five specifically reported miracles, plus the mention of supernatural acts involving numerous individuals.

Some may charge that we are arguing in a circle, but we have tried to show in this chapter that the acceptance of a universe run by natural law does not preclude a belief in the possibility of the miraculous. Even with the supposed determinism of Newtonian physics, it is not necessary to capitulate to pure naturalism. It is presumptuous for a philosopher like Hume to insist on such a complete and omniscient record of human history and natural science that one can confidently demonstrate the absolute uniformity of natural law and the nonexistence of variables that might open the door to the miraculous. Moreover, with the advent of Quantum physics, we are let out of the supposed straitjacket of Newtonian physics and permitted to hold to indeterminism in at least some small events.

Then, on a purely lay, nonphilosophical level, we find it a little easier to believe in miracles today. Almost every week we are treated to some new "miracle" (marvel) of medicine—organ transplants, laser surgery, new procedures, and more. We were all amazed during the Gulf War at the sophistication of modern weaponry and battle tactics. We take space exploration for granted now. The Russians have an operational space station. This year we celebrated the United States's twenty-fifth anniversary of that marvelous moon landing. There seems to be no limit to the possibilities of what can and will be done with the computer and the coming so-called information highway. If finite human creatures can do all this and more, is it so hard to believe that a being greater than us can perform miracles?

Chapter 4

CAN I REALLY BELIEVE THAT JESUS CHRIST LIVED ON EARTH?

Did Jesus really live on earth? It sounds like a stupid question. Is not time divided into B.C. and A.D.—Before Christ and *Anno Domini* (in the year of the Lord)? Are not the books on our coffee tables filled with paintings of events in the life of Christ? And haven't countless poets and prose writers down through the ages immortalized His earthly life? Yes, but some atheists still claim that Jesus did not really live on earth. One of their best-known spokesmen repeated the assertion on a national radio broadcast a couple of years ago. Supposedly the belief that Jesus really lived on earth had its origin in myth.

If they wished, doubters could also argue that the practice of dating "in the year of the Lord" began rather late and is no justification for the historical Jesus. The prominent Roman monk, Dionysius Exiguus (A.D. 525), because of his calendar reckonings gets credit for introducing the practice. It was not until two centuries later that the Venerable Bede (who lived at the monastery of Jarrow in northeastern England) helped make it the common way of dating. The fact that it took many centuries to establish this method of reckoning time does not cast doubt on either its validity or the existence of Christ. Nor does the modern Israeli insistence on dating events B.C.E. (Before the Common Era) and C. E. (in the Common Era) negate Christ's existence, for they are simply trying to obliterate all recognition of Jesus as their Messiah.

As a matter of fact, the delayed change of dating systems is perfectly understandable. Certainly it had nothing to do with a developing myth or legend about the life and ministry of Christ on earth. In the earliest days of the church, Christians truly believed in the existence of Christ and considerable numbers died for Him during the great persecutions. The emperor Constantine undoubtedly believed in the existence of Christ because he was baptized in His name at the end of his life after previously legalizing Christianity. Moreover, he had his sons brought up as Christians. When the emperor Theodosius made Christianity the faith of the Roman Empire and started to persecute pagans, he also truly believed in the existence of Christ on earth.

For centuries it had been customary to date events in the year of the reigning emperor. When Christianity became *the* legal faith of the Empire, there was no reason to change the practice. But after Constantine moved the imperial capital from Rome to Constantinople in 330 and barbarians set up their kingdoms in the West during the fifth century, it was no longer appropriate or meaningful to date events in the year of the emperor. He no longer controlled the West, and barbarian sacks of Rome occurred in 410 and 455. Under the circumstances, it is understandable that churchmen of the West should seek a new and more durable means of chronological reckoning. Hence the efforts of Dionsius Exiguus in 525. In the more politically stable East the dating of events in the year of the emperor continued for a longer period of time.

BIBLICAL REFERENCES TO CHRIST

Perhaps the earliest recorded witness to Jesus' life on earth was that of the apostle Paul. "But that appears in the Bible," the scoffer objects, implying that truth claims that are based on the Bible rest on inferior evidence or at least are somewhat suspect. The denial of biblical evidence in general and Paul's testimony in particular is rather old hat today, however. As a result of modern discovery, the Pauline Epistles enjoy an increasing reputation for validity among critical scholars. And it is of no little significance that such an outstanding theological liberal as Shirley Jackson Case of the University of Chicago could declare early in this century (1928), "The genuineness of the principal Pauline epistles is among the most generally accepted conclusions of what may be called modern critical opinion."[1] Paul's testimony is especially valuable because he was a violent opponent of Christ and had to be convinced of the truth of Christ's activities and claims.

Paul had much to say about the earthly ministry of Christ. By way of illustration, he referred to His incarnation (Romans 1:3); His institution of the Lord's Supper (1 Corinthians 11:23–26); His provision of eternal life (Romans 5:15–21); His crucifixion (1 Corinthians 2:2; Galatians 2:20); and His death, burial, and resurrection (1 Corinthians 15:3–8). Paul's statements about the life of Christ are minimal, however, compared to those in the Gospels. Parenthetically it should be noted that very likely most of Paul's letters were "mailed" before the first Gospel was written.

Although the value of the testimony of the Gospels to the life and ministry of Jesus Christ has been disputed, critical opinion concerning them has been forced to beat a retreat in recent decades. Critics used to say that the

---

1 Shirley Jackson Case, The *Historicity of Jesus,* 2d ed. (Chicago: University of Chicago Press, 1928), 178.

Gospels came into their present form long after Christ lived on earth, perhaps during the third century. By implication, or direct statement, critics taught that much of the information in the Gospels concerning Jesus was legendary, having developed during the century or two after His death. Now, however, on the basis of evidence from the papyri, we know that the New Testament was written in first-century Greek. An indication of the change in scholarly opinion appears in the declaration of such an outstanding liberal theologian and archaeologist as Millar Burrows (formerly of Yale): "it is evident . . . that the books of the New Testament were written in the first century."[2]

Sir Frederic Kenyon, former director of the British Museum, placed the date of the gospel of John near the end of the first century and the rest of the gospels about the time of the fall of Jerusalem (A. D. 70).[3] An eminent New Testament scholar, John A. T. Robinson, of Trinity College, Cambridge, in 1977 reversed himself on many of his earlier radical views and concluded that all the New Testament books were written between A.D. 47 and 70,[4] dates that are earlier than most conservatives would suggest. Having been written so soon after the events they record, the Gospels should be reliable in content. At least, many who knew Jesus would still have been alive and could have contested any errors of fact in the gospel narratives.

ROMAN LITERARY REFERENCES TO CHRIST

While we see that the biblical testimony concerning the historical Jesus has taken on increased validity, we also see

2 Millar Burrows, *What Mean These Stones?* (New Haven: American Schools of Oriental Research, 1941), 54.

3 Frederic Kenyon, *The Bible and Archaeology* (New York: Harper, 1940), 288.

4 John A. T. Robinson, Can We *Trust the New Testament?* (Grand Rapids: Eerdmans, 1977), 63.

that there is supporting evidence in several early Roman and Jewish sources for the historical Jesus. One of the earliest Romans to comment on the person of Christ was Tacitus (A. D. c. 60–c. 120). An orator and a politician, he is best known as a historian. The *Annals*, one of his historical works, is of particular importance for the present investigation. Written near the end of Tacitus' life, it contains a history of the Julian emperors from Tiberius to Nero (A. D. 14–68). In the section on Nero, Tacitus briefly describes the persecution of Christians, and in the process names their leader: "Christus, from whom their name is derived, was executed at the hands of the procurator Pontius Pilate in the reign of Tiberius."[5]

Pliny the Younger (A. D. c. 62–c. 113), while governor of Bithynia and Pontus in Asia Minor (modern Turkey), was faced with the issue of how to treat Christians, who were by then an illegal sect. About A .D. 111 or 112 he wrote to the emperor Trajan for advice on the subject. In describing Christians he said:

> But they declared that the sum of their guilt or error had amounted only to this, that on an appointed day they had been accustomed to meet before daybreak, and to recite a hymn antiphonally to Christ, as to God, and to bind themselves by an oath, not for the commission of any crime but to abstain from theft, robbery, adultery, and breach of faith, and not to deny a deposit when it was claimed.[6]

While this does not provide any detail concerning the person of Christ, it does attest to His existence—at least as far as these early Christians were concerned.

When Pliny went to Asia Minor to serve as governor of Bithynia and Pontus, he took along as his correspondent

---

5   Tacitus, *Annals* 15.44.

6   Pliny the Younger, *Correspondence of Trajan,* Epp. 10.96.

the biographer and historian Suetonius (A. D. c. 75–160). Suetonius' cheif work was the *Lives of the Caesars* (Julius to Domitian), of which only fragments remain. In his *Life of Claudius* appears this statement, "Since the Jews were continually making disturbances at the instigation of Chrestus, he [Claudius] expelled them from Rome."[7]

The interpretation of this passage in its context must be either that a disturbance had been caused by a Jew named Chrestus, who was living in Rome at the time, or that a controversy had arisen between Jews and Christians over Christ and certain doctrinal issues. Many accept the latter and feel that this is a testimony to the existence of Christ as early as the middle of the first century. Both the Greek and Latin words for Christian sometimes are spelled with an *e* rather than an *i* in New Testament manuscripts, and it is possible that *Christus* was also sometimes spelled *Chrestus*. That Claudius did expel the Jews from Rome is confirmed in Acts 18:2.

Another Roman witness to the person of Jesus Christ is Lucian of Samosata in Syria (A.D. c. 125–c. 190), whom many regard as the most brilliant writer of revived Greek literature under the Roman Empire. In his later years he held a government post in Egypt. Of particular interest to us is his satire on Christians and their faith, published under the title *The Passing of Peregrinus,* about 170. He describes Christ as the originator of "this new cult" of Christianity and mentions that he was "crucified in Palestine" for having originated the cult.[8]

JEWISH REFERENCES TO CHRIST

Greatest of the early Jewish historians was Josephus (A. D. c. 37–100). Among his writings were the *History of the Jewish War, Antiquities of the Jews,* an *Autobiography* and

---

7 Suetonius, *Life of Claudius,* 25.4.

8 Lucian, *Passing of Peregrinus* 1.11.13.

Against Apion. In the *Antiquities,* finished in A.D. 93, a much-disputed passage describes Jesus Christ:

> Now there was about this time Jesus, a wise man, if it be lawful to call him a man; for he was a doer of wonderful works, a teacher of such men as receive the truth with pleasure. He drew over to him both many of the Jews and many of the Gentiles. He was [the] Christ. And when Pilate, at the suggestion of the principal men amongst us, had condemned him to the cross, those that loved him at the first did not forsake him; for he appeared to them alive again the third day; as the divine prophets had foretold these and ten thousand other wonderful things concerning him. And the tribe of Christians, so named from him, are not extinct at this day.[9]

Obviously, this is a rather evangelical-sounding statement for a Jew of Josephus' standing to have made. Some have held, therefore, that the entire passage is an insertion made by a Christian; and the fourth-century church historian Bishop Eusebius of Caesarea has been suggested as the one responsible. But, it is now commonly believed that Josephus probably made some reference to the existence of Jesus in this passage and that we have here a doctored-up account rather than a complete interpolation. Some have even tried to restore the Josephus passage to its original wording.

In this connection, Professors Shlomo Pines and David Flusser of the Hebrew University in Jerusalem have reported on a tenth-century Arabic manuscript that contains a rendering of the debated passage very different from the traditional one. The Arabic rendering, which they believe to be the original, reads as follows:

---

9   Josephus, *Antiquities* 18.3.3.

At this time there was a wise man who was called Jesus. And his conduct was good, and [he] was known to be virtuous. And many people from among the Jews and other nations became his disciples. Pilate condemned him to be crucified and to die. And those who had become his disciples did not abandon his discipleship. They reported that he had appeared to them three days after his crucifixion and that he was alive; accordingly, he was perhaps the messiah concerning whom the prophets have recounted wonders.[10]

Whether or not this wording is Josephus' exact original is beside the point. It hardly seems possible that a person of Josephus' breadth of knowledge could have avoided completely a reference to Jesus of Nazareth in a reasonably complete history of the Jews. Moreover, later on in his account he spoke of James as "the brother of Jesus, who was called Christ."[11] This unembellished statement has a ring of authenticity and may be accepted as a bona fide confirmation of Jesus' life on earth.

Early Jewish tradition also confirms the existence of Jesus of Nazareth. The code of religious law, called "the traditions of the elders" or the Mishnah, was compiled about A.D. 200. Thereafter, a commentary called the Gamarah grew up around it. Together the Mishnah and the Gamarah are usually known as the Talmud, and the Babylonian form of the Talmud is longer than the Jerusalem form. The Talmud makes a number of hostile references to Jesus—most of them speak of Him as "One" who did such and such. One of the more specific allusions to Jesus appears in the tractate Sanhedrin (43a) of the Babylonian Talmud:

---

10 Peter Gross, "New Evidence on Jesus' Life Reported," *New York Times,* 13 February 1972, 1, 24.

11 Josephus, *Antiquities*, 20.9.1.

On the eve of the Passover, Jesus of Nazareth was hung. During forty days a herald went before him crying aloud: "He ought to be stoned because he has practiced magic, has led Israel astray and caused them to rise in rebellion. Let him who has something to say in his defence come forward and declare it." But no one came forward, and he was hung on the eve of the Passover.

This passage clearly attests Jesus' existence, implies His miraculous work ("practiced magic"), and indirectly refers to His death by crucifixion ("hung") rather than the usual execution by stoning.

In the light of all this assured or apparent testimony to the historicity of Jesus, skepticism has had to beat a retreat. In whatever way scholars or popular interpreters may evaluate the person of Jesus today, rarely will one ever completely deny His existence.[12]

---

12 For other defense of the historicity of Jesus, see Gary R. Habermas, *The Verdict of History* (Nashville: Thomas Nelson, 1988); Josh McDowell and Bill Wilson, *He Walked Among Us* (San Bernardino, Calif.: Here's Life Publishers, 1988); Josh McDowell, *Evidence That Demands a Verdict*, vol 1 (San Bernardino, Calif.: Here's Life Publishers, 1972); and E. M. Blaiklock, *Who Was Jesus?* (Chicago: Moody Press, 1974).

CAN I REALLY BELIEVE THAT JESUS IS GOD?

It seems preposterous on the face of it that we should be expected to worship a human being as God. Yet that is exactly what Christianity expects of all who would become Christians—that they worship Jesus as God. And if we do not worship Him as God, there is no hope for humanity. There is now no great doubt that Jesus lived on earth, or that He was crucified in Jerusalem early in the first century. But if we hold that He died for our sins, He had to be God. This is so because one might die to pay the penalty for himself or another or even for a small group, but not for everyone. For Jesus' death to be effective for all, however, His humanity had to be linked to deity with its infinite qualities. Then, as the God-man, He could die for all.

Any argument for Jesus' deity is linked to the inspiration of Scripture and a belief in the miraculous (chapters 2 and 3). A defense of His deity comes primarily from the Bible, and His ability to exercise control over all of nature is a powerful defense of His deity. In the West, generally in a court of law, a defendant who is on trial is presumed innocent until proven guilty, or in certain kinds of cases his position is accepted until his opponent proves otherwise. In the case of Jesus, who is accused of not being divine, we look first at His own claims, then at a host of witnesses, and finally at an evaluation of His actions.

JESUS' CLAIMS

To the Jews, who claimed Abraham as Father, Jesus asserted, "Before Abraham came to be, I am" (John 8:58, literal translation). By this Jesus taught there was a sense in which the idea of birth and beginning did not apply to Him; in Him was eternal existence (cf. Exodus 3:14). Further claim to eternity, an attribute of deity, appears in John 17, where Jesus referred to the glory He shared with the Father before the world came into being (vv. 5, 24).

Two of Jesus' claims concerning His ministry also indicate deity: the power to forgive sins, and the power of resurrection. His ability to forgive sins is clearly stated in the narrative of the healing of the palsied man. On that occasion Jesus said, "The Son of man hath power on earth to forgive sins" (Mark 2:10 KJV). And the scribes said. "Who can forgive sins but God only?" (Mark 2:7 KJV). Jesus promised resurrection to everyone who receives Him as Savior, "I will raise him up at the last day" (John 6:40 KJV). As Paul made clear in the argument of 1 Corinthians 15, the resurrection of believers is based on the resurrection of Christ. And Jesus avers that He has power to rise from the dead, as well as to raise others: "I lay down my life, that I might take it again. No man taketh it from me, but I lay it down of myself. I have power to lay it down, and I have power to take it again" (John 10:17–18 KJV). Only God can give life to the dead.

In a number of references, Jesus also asserts that God is His Father (Matthew 7:21; 10:32–33; 11:27; 12:50; 15:13; 16:17; 18:10, 19, 35; 20:23; 25:34; 26: 29, 53; Luke 2:49; 10:22; 22:29; 24:49; John 6:37–40, 57; and 10:35–36). That this is tantamount to a claim to deity is obvious from John 5:17–18 (KJV): "But Jesus answered them, My Father worketh hitherto, and I work. Therefore the Jews sought the more to kill him, because he not only had broken the sabbath, but said also that God was His Father, making himself equal with God." Last, Jesus equated Himself with God (John 14:9–10, 23; John 5:19–27). He does this especially in John 10:30, "I and my Father are one." *One* is neuter in the Greek, not masculine, indicating that they were one in substance or essence, not one person.

WITNESSES TO THE DEITY OF JESUS

Testimony of the Father

Jesus frequently spoke of His relationship to the Father and of the Father's interest in what the Son was doing on earth. On two occasions the Father rent the heavens and gave audible witness to this divine relationship. At Jesus' baptism He declared, "This is My beloved Son, in whom I am well pleased" (Matthew 3:17 NKJV; cf. Mark 1:11; Luke 3:22). Similarly, at the Transfiguration He asserted, "This is My beloved Son, in whom I am well pleased. Hear him" (Matthew 17:5 NKJV; cf. Mark 9:7; Luke 9:35).

Realization of the Disciples

While the disciples were slow to grasp the full significance of Jesus' nature, on occasion they did recognize His deity. After the incident of His walking on the water and Peter's attempt to do the same, the disciples in the boat worshiped, saying, "Truly You are the Son of God" (Matthew 14:33 NKJV). They affirmed this at the time of Peter's great confession, "You are the Christ, the Son of the living God" (Matthew 16:16 NKJV). And after the resurrection, Doubting Thomas, when confronted by the risen Christ, bowed in adoration, "My Lord and my God" (John 20:28 NKJV).

Testimony of John the Baptist

All four of the Gospels record briefly the ministry of John the Baptist, the forerunner of Jesus, who spoke about

Him in exalted terms (*see* Matthew 3:1–17; Mark 1:3–8; Luke 3:2–20; John 1:15–36). But in the gospel of John, he specifically described Jesus as divine: "Behold! The Lamb of God who takes away the sin of the world!" (1:29 NKJV); "And I have seen and testified that this is the Son of God" (1:34 NKJV).

Acknowledgment of Satanic Forces

Even the demons recognized the deity of Jesus and His authority over them. Evidence of this surfaced on two occasions when Jesus healed demon-possessed individuals. At Capernaum a demon cried out, "What have we to do with You, Jesus of Nazareth? Did You come to destroy us? I know who You are—the Holy One of God" (Mark 1:24 NKJV). The demons at Gadara agonized, "What have we to do with You, Jesus, You Son of God? Have You come here to torment us before the time? (Matthew 8:29 NKJV).

Witness of Scripture in General

Evidence from His Names

The names given to the God-Man in the Gospels are not empty titles. Each has significance. Several indicate deity. As the *Logos* (or Word), John 1:1–3, He is the expression or revealer of God. That the *Logos* is not some inferior being who merely conveys an impression of God to humanity is clear from the first verses of John's gospel, where He is declared to be *eternal* and *God Himself.*

Although *Son of Man* does not always indicate deity, sometimes it does. For instance, as Son of Man, He has authority on earth to forgive sins (Matthew 9:6), to execute judgment (John 5:27), to send His angels to gather the tares (Matthew 13:41), to sit on the throne of His glory (Matthew 19:28; 25:31), and to come again (Matthew 24:44; 26:64). When He announced that He was the Son of Man whom Daniel declared, the high priest recognized this as a claim to deity and accused Him of blasphemy (Matthew 26:63–64; cf. Daniel 7:13). Again, the application of *Son of God* to Him does not always indicate deity. And of course we are called sons and daughters of God by faith in Christ. But clearly calling Him the Son of God normally did mean that He was divine. For example, as the divine Son, He is said to execute all judgment (John 5:22), to have life in Himself and to quicken whom He will (John 5:21, 26), and to give eternal life (John 10:10)—all divine prerogatives.

Although *Lord* is used in various ways in the New Testament, sometimes it is applied to Christ in such a way as to be practically the equivalent of *God*. The apostle Thomas addressed Him as Lord and God (John 20:28). The apostle Paul told the Philippian jailer that for salvation he should believe on the "Lord Jesus Christ" (Acts 16:31). The Christmas message announced a Savior "who is Christ the Lord" (Luke 2:11). Among other references, Acts 2:36 speaks of Jesus as "Lord and Christ." In yet other passages Jesus is simply called *God*. For example, Titus 2:13 speaks of "our great God and Savior, Christ Jesus." Elsewhere, God said to the Son, "Thy throne, 0 God, is forever and ever, and the righteous scepter is the scepter of His kingdom" (Hebrews 1:8 NASB). Peter writes of "our God and Savior, Jesus Christ" (2 Peter 1:1 NKJV), and 1 John 5:20 (NKJV) reads, "in His Son Jesus Christ. This is the true God, and eternal life."

Evidence from Messianic Expectation and Fulfillment

The Old Testament is full of prophecies about a coming Messiah who would rescue Israel from her sins and ultimately bring in an age of glory. Of special importance to our present study are three passages in Isaiah. In Isaiah 7:14 there appears the prophecy that He would be virgin born and that His name would be *Immanuel*, which means "God with us." Subsequently, Isaiah predicted that Messiah would be called "mighty God" and "everlasting Father" (9:6), another clear statement of deity. Then Isaiah prophesied the coming of a forerunner of the Messiah, who would "make straight in the desert a highway for our God" (Isaiah 40:3 NKJV). The forerunner was obviously John the Baptist, who announced Christ (Matthew 3:1–6). Matthew 1:22–23 specifically states that the Virgin Birth was fulfilled in the incarnation of Christ, and that He was Immanuel, meaning "God with us." Much more could be said about Messianic prophecy and its fulfillment, but it is enough at this point to mention James Smith's new five-hundred-page study, *What the Bible Teaches About the Promised Messiah,* a treatment of seventy-three key Old Testament prophecies about the Messiah. The Old Testament predicted that the Messiah would be truly divine, and the New Testament declares that that prophecy was fulfilled in Christ.

Evidence from His Attributes

Theologians often talk about the attributes of God, by which they simply mean His inherent characteristics or qualities. While the list they construct is fairly long, a few are uniquely divine, and Jesus' possession of them helps to support His deity. They are eternity, omnipresence, omniscience, omnipotence, and immutability. His eternity we have already commented about; the others require comment here.

Omnipresence simply means everywhere present. He was in heaven while on earth: "the Son of man which is in heaven" (John 3:13 KJV). And since the Ascension He is on earth while He is in heaven. As part of the Great Commission He promised, "I am with you always" (Matthew 28:20). And during this age whenever two or three are gathered in Jesus name, He is there among them (Matthew 18:20). Moreover, Christ dwells in all believers, and that fact brings assurance of believers' spending eternity with God: "Christ in you, the hope of glory" (Colossians 1:27 KJV).

Jesus, *omniscience,* His knowing all things, was recognized by the disciples: "Now we are sure that You know all things." They also observed that His omniscience was evidence of His deity: "By this we believe that You came forth from God" (John 16:30 NASB). Later, Peter, in a private conversation with Jesus also testified, "You know all things" (John 21:17 NASB). Some specific examples of His omniscience in action include knowing what was in man (John 2:24–25), knowing the life history of the Samaritan woman (John 4:29), knowing the one who would betray Him (John 6:70–71), and knowing the time and manner of His leaving this world (John 12:33; 13:1). There are some problems with the acceptance of this attribute, however, chief of which was His ignorance of the date of His return (Mark 13:32). The only reasonable explanation for this lack on His part is that, while on earth, He subjected Himself to certain human limitations; now He *must* know the date.

Jesus' *omnipotence* involves His power over all things. The comprehensiveness of the term appears especially in the Great Commission that states that all power or authority had been given to Him (Matthew 28:18) and in His sustaining power: He upholds "all things by the word of His power" (Hebrews 1:3 NKJV). In His ministry on earth, Jesus demonstrated by His miraculous works His power over all things. This is clear from subsequent discussion of His activities.

Finally, Jesus is *immutable* or unchanging, not fickle in His plans, promises and person. The classic verse to express this attribute is Hebrews 13:8: "Jesus Christ is the same yesterday, today, and forever" (NASB).

Evidence from Certain Relationships

Jesus is put on a par with the Father and the Holy Spirit in the baptismal formula (Matthew 28:19) and in the apostolic benediction of 1 Corinthians 13:14. He is the image of God (Colossians 1:15). Whatever the Father has belongs also to Him (John 16:15). He and the Father act together in abiding with the believer (John 14:23).

Other Evidence from Inspired Scripture.

In addition to the foregoing evidence for the deity of Christ, New Testament witness adds other items of value. Of all the Gospels, John's gives the most exalted view of the person of Christ. As noted, Jesus has always existed (1:1); He is God (1:1), and has enjoyed eternal and intimate fellowship with the Father (1:2, 18). He is the only begotten of the Father, has become incarnate, and made provision for the salvation of humanity (1:14; 3:16–18). Constantly in his gospel and first epistle, John affirms that He is the Son of God, the Light of the world, and the Savior. Paul calls Him the Lord of glory (1 Corinthians 2:8), and the "Son of God" who "gave himself for me" (Galatians 2:20 KJV). Paul also says that Jesus is "equal with God" (Philippians 2:6 KJV), and that "in Him dwells all the fullness of the Godhead bodily" (Colossians 2:9 NKJV). The writer to the Hebrews describes Him both as God's Son (1:2) and as God (1:8). Certainly the New Testament leaves no doubt of His deity.

AN EXAMINATION OF JESUS' ACTIONS

In establishing a case for Jesus' deity, it is necessary first to examine His claims, then to look at the massive testimony in support of His claims, and finally to observe how He conducted Himself in human relations. Much of this information appears in the claims He made or in His ability to read the minds of those with whom He spoke. But there is the additional dimension of the demonstration of His power in miraculous acts. The thirty-five miracles described in the Gospels (in addition to numbers of miracles not specified) may be grouped into seven categories, demonstrating Jesus' power over all of creation. Although most of these miracles appear in more than one gospel, only one reference is given here to avoid a massive catalog of Scripture.

(1) He healed diseases for which there was no known cure or provided instant healing without the person's having to go through recuperation: healing Peter's mother-in-law (Matthew 8:14–17); cleansing a leper in Galilee (Matthew 8:2–4); healing a woman with an issue of blood (Matthew 9:20–22); healing a man with dropsy (Luke 14:1–6); and cleansing ten lepers in Samaria (Luke 17:11–19).

(2) He healed at a distance or by "remote control," without even seeing the afflicted: healing a nobleman's son at Cana (John 4:46–54); and healing a centurion's servant at Capernaum (Matthew 8:5–13).

(3) He restored limbs or body functions: healing a lame man at the Pool of Bethesda (John 5:1–9); restoring a paralytic in Capernaum (Matthew 9:2–8); healing a man with a withered hand (Matthew 12:9–14); healing two blind men (Matthew 9:27–31); healing a deaf mute in Decapolis (Mark 7:31–37); healing a blind man at Bethsaida (Mark 8:22–26); healing a man born blind (John 9:1–7); healing a crippled woman (Luke 13:10–17); healing blind Bartimaeus (Matthew 20:29–34); and restoring Malchus' ear (Luke 22:49–51).

(4) He exhibited power over victuals: turning water into wine (John 2:1–11); feeding five thousand (Matthew 14:14–21); and feeding four thousand (Matthew 15:32–39).

(5) He exercised power over nature: stilling a storm on the Sea of Galilee (Matthew 8:18, 23–27); walking on the water (Matthew 14:24–33); cursing a fig tree (Matthew 21:18–19); providing two miraculous catches of fish (Luke 5:1–11; John 21:1–14); and finding tribute money (Matthew 17:24–27).

(6) He wielded power over demons: delivering a synagogue demoniac (Mark 1:23–28); healing a blind and dumb demoniac (Matthew 12:22); delivering the Gadarene demoniac (Matthew 8:28–34); delivering a dumb demoniac (Matthew 9:32–33); delivering the Syrophoenician's daughter

(Matthew 15:21–28); and delivering a demon-possessed boy (Matthew 17:14–18).

(7) He demonstrated power over death: raising a widow's son (Luke 7:11–17); raising Jairus' daughter (Matthew 19:18–19, 23–26); and raising Lazarus (John 11:17-44).

WHY THE REJECTION OF JESUS' DEITY?

If Jesus was the divine wonder-worker on earth that this chapter portrays Him to have been, why is there such a debate about who He was and what He did? And why is there such a rejection of His deity and His message? The apostle Paul succinctly gave the explanation for first–century opponents of Jesus; his explanations in large measure continue to the present. He said, first, that the preaching of Christ crucified was to the Jews a stumbling block or offense and to the Greeks, Greco-Romans or Gentiles, foolishness (1 Corinthians 1:23). The first-century Jews were expecting a Messiah but not one who would especially meet their spiritual needs. Increasingly they longed for a Messiah who would be a political deliverer, who would rescue them from Rome's domination. They wanted a Messiah who would come in power, not in meekness and not one who would subject Himself to the humiliation of the Cross. They stumbled over the concept of a divine Messiah who would, in love, pay the penalty for their sins. Not only was the idea of a political Messiah gaining prominence in Jewish thought, but also an emphasis on law-keeping and righteous standing before the law was becoming increasingly entrenched. So, they stumbled over the concept of a divine Messiah's providing for them salvation by grace.

The first-century Greeks, Greco-Romans or Gentiles, considered Jesus' message "foolishness." The Greco–Roman world respected power, whether the military power of the Roman army, or the political power of the bureaucracy, or the economic power of the entrenched aristocracy.

Deity they could accept, and they worshiped their emperor, but a divine power figure should not act in humility, should not subject Himself to the maltreatment of others in the process of providing salvation—that was foolishness. Moreover, Greeks of a more philosophical bent (not all Greeks were philosophical in orientation) were turned off by a self-effacing gospel that did not call on people to do something to establish standing with God and that did not put a premium on a high-flung philosophical orientation or a sophisticated, intellectual approach to religion.

Second, Paul observed that non-Christians are spiritually "dead" in their sins (Ephesians 2:1). They cannot even wiggle. In other words, they can do nothing to achieve a standing before God. The position of their not being able to do anything is too humiliating for most; they want to think they can do something to earn their way to heaven.

Third, Paul observed that Satan actually "energizes" unbelievers (Ephesians 2:2, translated "works in" in most versions), and blinds their minds "lest the light of the gospel of the glory of Christ, who is the image of God, should shine on them" (2 Corinthians 4:4 NASB). Thus, there is a sinister effort afoot to prevent people from believing that Jesus Christ is very God and that the salvation He provided is a valid option for those seeking salvation. The howl set up by the masses of Jews and Gentiles against the divine Christ in the first century has continued down through the ages. The simple faith He requires is a stumbling block to those who want to earn their way into heaven by doing and being good and to those who are so obsessed by power that they cannot understand or accept a salvation offered by the Potentate of the universe who presented Himself in meekness and love.

He could have come in power and glory to a dying world in the first century. He told Peter in the Garden of Gethsemane that He could have twelve legions of angels (sixty thousand) at His command if He wished (Matthew 26:53).

There were plenty of angels around at His birth (Luke 2:13). What could have occurred at Jesus' first coming is frighteningly portrayed in the description of His second coming in Revelation 19:11–21 when He descends to deal with the wicked. But if Jesus had come in power and glory instead of in humility and grace at His first coming, there would be no plan of salvation and none of us would escape the judgment.

Chapter 6

CAN I REALLY BELIEVE THAT JESUS ROSE FROM THE DEAD?

Every Easter from Christian pulpits all over the world goes forth the exultant shout, "He is risen!" And frequently the congregations respond, "He is risen indeed!" Television programs throughout the West and even in Russia report the celebration of Jesus' resurrection from the dead. Church bells peal in the Vatican, Jerusalem, and elsewhere. Even in China, the Government periodically permits groups to hold Easter sunrise services at the Great Wall. In America, where polls can be taken with some degree of accuracy, about two-thirds reportedly believe in the resurrection of Jesus with "absolute certainty."[1]

But what about the other third of Americans and the untold millions elsewhere who either waver in their belief in the Resurrection or outright deny it? The modern, scien-

---

1 A Gallup Poll taken in 1978 showed that almost two-thirds of Americans believed in the resurrection of Jesus with "absolute certainty," and it does not appear that there has been a substantial shift in numbers since then.

tific worldview leads people to deny the possibility of divine intervention in human history. Miracles are ruled out in advance, and in the face of apparently reliable claims of the Resurrection, theories are concocted to explain how witnesses were deluded. Nonbelievers often become adherents to one of these theories and believers are sometimes troubled by them. On close examination, however these theories lose their punch and most of them wither away altogether.

NON-CHRISTIAN THEORIES OF THE RESURRECTION

Stolen-Body Theory

The stolen-body theory circulated immediately after the Resurrection. Members of the guard posted to watch the tomb of Jesus went to the chief priests and reported what had happened. The Jewish religious leadership then gave a large sum of money to the soldiers with the instructions, "You are to say, 'His disciples came by night and stole Him away while we were asleep.' And if this should come to the governor's ears, we will win him over and keep you out of trouble" (Matthew 28:12–13, NASB). Thereafter the story spread abroad and continues to the present that the disciples stole the body of Jesus and then preached the Resurrection. Viewed from the standpoint of the intervention of either friend or foe, this theory seems impossible. Would Jesus' enemies do the very thing most likely to spread the story of His resurrection? And would not they have produced His body when the disciples did preach the Resurrection? If Jesus' friends had wished to steal the body, could they have? There was the stone, the seal, and the guard.

Could a group of unarmed or lightly armed and militarily untrained disciples, without body armor, have defeated seasoned, well-armed Roman soldiers? Not without creating so much noise and confusion that a crowd would have gathered.

Could the disciples have broken the seal and moved the stone? Not without great difficulty. Tombstones were not easy to move. The usual rolling stone (shaped like a dough-nut) that was used to close a tomb was rolled into a downwardly inclined trough and dropped into a slot to cover the tomb's entrance. Once the stone was in place, it took great effort to move it, even if there was no seal.

Could the disciples have hidden Jesus' body? Not likely. It would have been necessary for them to have taken Jesus' body out and carry it off somewhere. By the time they had fought with the guards and had rolled the stone away, there would have been a considerable crowd to witness the event. It would have been impossible for the disciples to have taken the body away secretly or to have hidden it secretly.

Would the disciples, in their haste, have taken the time to unwind the bands of embalming cloth from His body and leave them in the tomb, as the gospel narrative indicates was the case (John 20:6–7)? Not if He was still dead. It would have been totally inappropriate to disturb His burial wrappings. We may infer but not dogmatically declare that the burial cloth, somewhat stiffened by various spices, remained in the form of a body after the Resurrection; thus the burial cloth was not unwrapped.

That the soldiers would report the theft of Jesus' body while they slept is laughable. In the first place, if true, such a dereliction of duty made them liable to court-martial and severe punishment or death. Second, if they were sleeping they would not know who stole the body. Third, it is incomprehensible that they all would have slept long enough and soundly enough for the disciples to break the seal (requiring hammering?) and with great effort to move the stone. Fourth, the fact that a simple bribe would be sufficient to get the soldiers off the hook implies that something strange happened, and they were not guilty of some failure on their part that was worthy of court-martial after all.

If the disciples had been successful in stealing Jesus' body, would they have preached the Resurrection with such convincing power? This falsehood would always have been a burden on their consciences, with the accompanying dread that one of their number might betray the secret. As someone has said, "Hypocrites do not become martyrs. They might have been deluded, but they were not liars." Certainly it is established from Scripture and history that the disciples were convinced of the resurrection of Jesus Christ. And it was the Resurrection that accounts for the radical change in the disciples after Jesus' death.

Alternatively, if Jesus' enemies had stolen the body (if they could have), they would have produced it when Christians began to talk about the Resurrection. And with Jesus' dead body on display, His enemies would have nipped Christianity in the bud. As a matter of fact, the stolen-body theory has been discredited and revived periodically throughout history and is not now widely held.

The Swoon Theory

Some have tried to get around the resurrection of Jesus by suggesting that He did not really die, but merely lapsed into a temporary coma or swooned as a result of His physical sufferings. He then recovered in the cool, damp tomb. Such a theory is harder to believe than the biblical account and gives rise to a flood of questions. How could Jesus, in His weakened condition, have pushed the heavy stone from the tomb's entrance? How could He have escaped the Roman guard to whom neglect of duty in such circumstances probably would have meant death? In His weak and wan condition how could He have convinced His disciples that He was indeed the Lord of glory for Whom they should be willing to jeopardize their lives? Where did

He finally disappear to and die in anonymity? How could He go off to some solitary retreat, unknown to the most attached of His disciples, when they, because of great persecution and trial, were dependent on His aid?

What about His sufferings. Had He not collapsed while carrying His cross? Had He not suffered nail wounds in His hands and feet? Had He not hung on the cross for an extended time of suffering? Had not the Roman soldiers, familiar with such a form of punishment, pronounced Him dead? Did not the soldiers ram his side with a spear to make sure he was dead—causing blood and water to gush forth (John 19: 33–34)? Did not Pilate order his soldiers to make sure Jesus was dead before permitting His burial (Mark 15:44–45)? Would not Joseph of Arimathea and Nicodemus have been sure of His death before burying Him? After discussing the Crucifixion and the piercing of Jesus' side, an analysis in the *Journal of the American Medical Society* concluded: "Interpretations based on the assumption that Jesus did not die on the cross appear to be at odds with modern medical knowledge."[2]

If Jesus merely swooned, He must have been bodily the same after the Resurrection as before, which was not the case. Moreover, if He did not rise from the dead, our Lord permitted the Gospel message to be founded on a hoax, which is entirely contrary to His nature and approach. If He merely swooned, He not only made the apostles base deceivers in preaching the Resurrection as being the basis of the Christian faith, but also He was a party to their deception.

Finally, a swoon would be meaningless. Jesus came into the world to save sinners. God had set up a system of animal sacrifices in the Old Testament as a temporary handling of sin until a "once-for-all-sacrifice" should be

---

2   *The Journal of the American Medical Society* 255, no. 11 (March 1986): 1463.

made. John the Baptist announced Jesus as the "Lamb of God, which taketh away the sin of the world" (John 1:29, 36 KJV). Peter described Him as a "lamb without blemish and without spot" (1 Peter 1:19 KJV). And Revelation speaks of Him as the "Lamb slain from the foundation of the world" (Revelation 13:8 KJV). Adam incurred *death* because of his sin and brought death on all humanity. Jesus as the second Adam *tasted death* for all and then defeated death in the Resurrection. "For as in Adam all die, even so in Christ shall all be made alive" (1 Corinthians 15:22 KJV); "and if Christ has not been raised, your faith is worthless; you are still in your sins" (1 Corinthians 15:17 NASB).

The Passover Plot

Somewhat related to the swoon theory is the passover plot, concocted by Hugh Schonfield in a novel by that name (1967). Although it is not a theory of long standing like the others described in this chapter, it has stirred up enough interest to require some comment here. This is the story of Jesus' conspiring, especially with Joseph of Arimathea and Lazarus, to convince His disciples that He was the Messiah. So, He manipulated events to make it appear that He fulfilled prophecies concerning the Messiah. He planned to pretend death and to revive later. The passover plot collapsed, however, when the unexpected happened: a Roman soldier thrust his spear in Jesus' side and the conspiracy was foiled. When the Crucifixion proved fatal, the coconspirators had to dispose of Jesus' body, leaving the disciples to account for the empty tomb. The supposed appearances of Jesus are presented as cases of mistaken identity.

As with the swoon theory, this plot violates the high moral character of Jesus and turns Him into a messianic pretender who deceived even His closest disciples—a highly unlikely achievement. Moreover, if a pretender, Jesus could hardly have manipulated many of the messianic prophecies (e. g., where He was born, Micah 5:2) or reactions of others to Him (e. g., John the Baptist's announcement of Him, Matthew 3). There was also the problem of getting past the soldiers to steal His body. Too many people under various circumstances saw Jesus and His crucifixion wounds for these appearances to be written off as cases of mistaken identity. Finally, there are the major questions of how the conspirators disposed of the body and convinced people that the Resurrection really happened.

The Wrong-Tomb Theory

This is the view that Mary Magdalene and the other women went to the wrong tomb in the darkness of the early morning hours of resurrection Sunday. When they found it empty, in error they reported the Resurrection. This is a very weak theory because Jewish and Roman authorities could have gone to the right tomb later in the day and produced the body to set matters straight; they did not do so. Note the bribe to the soldiers (Matthew 28:11–15), which eliminates any question about incorrect identification of the tomb. There was no chance that they would have taken such action if there was any doubt in their minds about the identity of the tomb. Moreover, Peter and John went to the tomb in broad daylight and saw it open and the empty grave clothes lying there. In answering this theory, it is important to note that the women themselves wanted to be sure of going to the right tomb for the proper anointing of the body. They had noted the tomb and the burial on Friday before the onset of the Sabbath and then had gone off to prepare the ointments (Luke 23:55–56).

The Vision Theory

According to this view, Jesus really appeared to His disciples after His death but only in spiritual visions—though they took the form of bodily appearances.

117

But, if it is admitted that Jesus really appeared to His disciples in visions, the door has been opened to the miraculous; and why not just as well admit a real resurrection, as the Scripture indicates? This view is based on the assertion that Mary Magdalene, an excitable woman,[3] had a vision of the resurrected Lord, and the disciples eagerly embraced the idea and passed it on, imagining that they also saw visions of Him. The whole business of the Resurrection is made to be merely a product of the subconscious.

Here again some questions are in order. If a product of the psychological makeup of the individual, a vision is merely a transference to the supposed reality of what has already taken possession of the mind; there is an excited expectation that the idea will somehow become a reality. But did Mary or the other women expect Him to arise? Did they not go to the tomb to anoint or embalm Him? (Mark 16:1). Did not Mary mistake Jesus for the gardener (John 20:15)? Did not the disciples at first refuse to believe Mary when she told them of the Resurrection? Also, is it not true that in a vision appearance the one viewed is shrouded in glory? Jesus in every instance appeared as a normal man. Are not visions usually fleeting things? Jesus spoke at length to numbers of disciples at one time. When individuals have visions that are a product of the mind or subconscious, do they stand up to their visions and say, "I don't believe it," as Thomas did (John 20:25)? The truth is that the disciples were in such a depressed state of mind before the Resurrection that subjective visions were the last thing in the world likely to befall them. And is it not strange that

---

3 There is no basis in fact for assuming that Mary was a nervous, excitable woman, given to "seeing things" because of the after effects of her demon possession. She had been completely and gloriously healed by the Lord and appeared as a tower of strength during the Passion Week when most of the disciples were not.

if Jesus' appearances were visions, they began within a few hours of rolling the stone back from the tomb, before legend or imagination had had a chance to develop, and after forty days (the time of the Ascension) they ceased forever?

The Spiritual-Only Theory

Many treat the Resurrection in a spiritual sense. Jesus became spiritually alive in the disciples' hearts. They were possessed by His spirit. And today, when individuals have an experience of faith, Christ becomes alive in them. So the Resurrection is constantly taking place. It is true that the Spirit took possession of the disciples after the Ascension and that the Spirit comes to indwell the hearts of believers today when they receive Christ by faith. But the resurrection of Jesus was to the early disciples an objective reality—upon which a spiritual experience was *based*. The subjective experience was not a substitute for the objective reality.

Scripture is clear in teaching that Jesus rose physically from the dead and that after the Resurrection He possessed a real body. He showed His hands and feet and told His disciples to handle Him to make sure it was He and not a spirit (Luke 24:39–40). He ate food in an upper room (Luke 24:41–43). He invited Thomas to put his hands in His wounds (John 20:27–28). He kindled a fire on the shore of the Sea of Galilee, broiled some fish, and distributed food to the hungry disciples (John 21:9–13).

TWO SPECIAL OBJECTIONS TO THE RESURRECTION

There are two special objections to the Resurrection or two supposed defects in the evidence for the Resurrection. The first is the lack of an eyewitness to the Resurrection. No one saw Jesus rise from the dead. One British theologian counters this argument by telling the story of a friend who had been on a journey, and who had returned home without his coming being seen by anyone in the family. When they found him in his room, they were delighted and of course did not doubt that it was he and that he had returned just because they did not see him return. Just so, the disciples knew Jesus had died and had been buried and now was beside them. He could not have been with them if He had not risen. The theologian suggests that if the disciples had seen Jesus arise, the critics would still not be satisfied. They would merely concoct theories to account for the disciples' "delusion," as there are now theories to explain away the Resurrection itself.[4]

The second supposed defect in our evidence is the apparent inconsistencies in the Gospel accounts of the Resurrection. Charles Perry, provost of the Episcopal Church's National Cathedral in Washington, states that the Gospel narratives "are wildly variant,"[5] implying that they are therefore somewhat unreliable or unhistorical or at least questionable. But no two writers see the same thing in exactly the same way. For example, a mother, a fireman, an insurance adjuster, and a social worker will describe a fire in a house down the block in quite different ways, but presumably all will agree on the essentials. The New Testament accounts of the Resurrection are singularly independent and provide us with narratives that fit the purpose and personalities of the writers. The fact that they are not slavishly repetitive gives them a ring of authenticity. As a matter of fact, all the testimonies agree as to the central points: Jesus died; was buried; a stone was placed at the entrance of the tomb, with a seal and an armed guard; on the third day, very early He came out of the tomb; He appeared to many during the next forty days; and then

---

4 William Milligan, *The Resurrection of Our Lord* (London: Macmillan, 1890), 55–56.

5 Peter Steinfels, "Jesus Died—And Then What Happened?" *The New York Times*, 3 April 1988, E9.

ascended to Heaven and was seen no more. The variations do not obscure the central core of the narrative.

EVIDENCE FOR THE RESURRECTION

There is not much debate anymore that Jesus lived on earth, or that He was put on trial or that He was crucified and died and was buried. Jesus died—and then what? Even such a secular publication as the *New York Times* has stated, "Shortly after Jesus was executed, his followers were suddenly galvanized from a baffled and cowering group into people whose message about a living Jesus and a coming kingdom, preached at the risk of their lives, eventually changed an empire. Something happened. . . . But exactly what?"[6]

Preaching of the Disciples

To begin with, it is important to note that the disciples's declaration that Jesus had risen was evidence of its actuality. After all, one of the charges against Jesus was that He had planned an insurrection against Rome. Those who at that time preached His resurrection and who evidently marched under His banner could have been charged with plotting a conspiracy and could have been imprisoned and executed for treason. Likewise, if Jesus was alive, His Jewish enemies would be put in a position of having killed their Messiah—a charge often voiced by early Christians (e. g., Acts 2:23, 36; 3:14–15; 4:10; 5:30–31). The disciples would hardly risk the wrath of either Rome or the Jewish establishment if they were not absolutely convinced of Jesus' resurrection.

---

6   Ibid., E1. The New Testament declares that what happened was the resurrection of Jesus and then goes on to give evidences supporting the actuality of that event.

Chapter 6

Material Facts Concerning the Resurrection

The Removed Stone

Support for the Resurrection also comes from material circumstances evident to contemporary observers. The first concerns the removed stone. The tomb was closed by a large stone; then the tomb was sealed and guarded by soldiers. The women who came to anoint Jesus' body with additional spices knew they could not move the stone (Mark 16:3) and were surprised to find it had been removed and the tomb opened. Although something has been said earlier about the stone, further comment is in order here. Ancient Palestinian tombs were commonly closed by large, circular stones, flat on both sides and weighing a ton or more. These stones were placed in a trough having a slight incline and a slot in front of the tomb opening. Once the stone was rolled in place, it could be moved only with considerable effort. (Jesus' tomb was closed in conventional fashion, Matthew 27:60). Such stones at tomb entrances may still be seen in East Jerusalem.

When the women arrived at the tomb, the stone had been moved—not just rolled to one side but lying flat and out of the trough (as the Greek indicates, Matthew 28:2; Luke 24:2). The guards reported that an earthquake had occurred and that an angel had not only moved the stone but also had sat on it (Matthew 28:2). There is no natural explanation for the moving of the stone. The women could not have done it (it was "extremely large," Mark 16:4) and indeed were shocked to find it moved. The disciples could not have moved it and have taken the body without an armed clash with the guard and witnesses. It is important to keep in mind that the tomb was a short distance from Golgotha (John 19:41), which was near the city and near a public execution place. The fact that the authorities apparently launched no further investigation hints that the report of the disciples' theft of the body was a smoke screen to cover the truth of the Resurrection.

The Empty Tomb

The empty tomb is also support for the Resurrection. The angels declared that the tomb was empty because Jesus had risen from the dead (Matthew 28:5–6). Mary Magdalene and Peter and John reported that the body was gone. It would have taken at least two men to remove the body, so there should have been witnesses. Who could have done so and why would they have done it? Certainly Roman or Jewish authorities would not have gotten in the way of their own plan to protect the body of Jesus. Tomb robbers would have no interest in the body if they had broken in and had not found any valuables. The disciples were totally surprised by the empty tomb and certainly were too demoralized, upset, and fearful of the authorities to have organized an effort to rescue the body from the hands of armed soldiers. Note that on resurrection night, when Jesus appeared to the assembled disciples, they were gathered behind locked doors "for fear of the Jews" (John 20:19).

The Graveclothes

As Joseph of Arimathea and Nicodemus prepared Jesus' body for burial, they did so in the customary way (John 19:39–40), which involved their winding bands of cloth around the body and using a generous supply of aromatic spices both as a preservative and to hold the bands of cloth together. Mark 15:46 (Greek text) says that Joseph "wound him in linen cloth" and that the pair used one-hundred pounds of spices in the process (John 19:40), until the body looked a little like an Egyptian mummy. Then, a square of cloth was wrapped around the head and tied under the chin.

When Peter and John entered the tomb, they saw the linen wrappings lying there (John 20:6) and the face cloth "rolled up" by itself (John 20:7). Certainly no grave robber would have taken the time to unwrap the body and carefully lay the wrappings where the body had been. Presumably they still appeared to have the form of the body in them. And the face cloth was not folded but "rolled up," as it might have surrounded the head. John "saw and believed" (v. 8), saw, meaning to "understand" or "realize" and believed "that Jesus had risen, passing through the graveclothes, which He left undisturbed as silent proof that death could not hold Him, nor material bonds restrain Him."[7]

Witness of the Physical Appearances of the Resurrected Jesus

When we begin to think about the New Testament accounts of Jesus' resurrection and of His appearances to numerous individuals, we need to remember that there were plenty of people still alive when the Gospels were written who had experienced or knew about the events they recorded.

Thus, they could contest any supposed errors or exaggerations. In fact, Paul specifically stated that of five hundred to whom Jesus appeared at once (see discussion below) most of them were still alive when he wrote 1 Corinthians in about A.D. 55 (1 Corinthians 15:6). This is not the place for a long discussion of when New Testament books were written, but conservatives commonly have long held that Matthew and Luke, at least (and Acts, which often refers to the resurrection), were written between about A.D. 50[8] and 60. Liberals have regularly been pulling

---

7 Merrill C. Tenney, *The Reality of the Resurrection* (Chicago: Moody, 1972), 119.

8 Recently three papyrus fragments of Matthew 26 were discovered in

down the dates of composition of New Testament books, and Bishop John A. T. Robinson, Anglican dean of chapel and professor at Cambridge, has now concluded that all New Testament books were written between about A.D. 47 and 70.[9] He puts the first draft of Mark's gospel as early as A.D. 45 (p. 73), only about a dozen years or so after the resurrection. Of course, not all follow Robinson's dating, but there is agreement among liberals and conservatives that at least some books alluding to the Resurrection were written while numbers of witnesses to the event were still alive.

According to the Gospels, Acts, and 1 Corinthians 15, there were twelve specific postresurrection appearances of Jesus, providing abundant evidence that He really had risen from the dead. They differ considerably in time, place, persons involved, and effects. The variety helps to demonstrate that His appearing was not confined to locale—to some predictable psychological situation or to any preconditions. So, opponents cannot explain away the appearances in terms of any of the usual psychological conditions or expectations. To confront modern psychological explanations, the manifestations, though differing in many ways (deliberately we may argue), agree unanimously that His resurrection was physical, not spiritual, because those to whom He appeared not only saw, heard, and touched Him but also even ate with Him.

Before discussing the individual appearances of the resurrected Jesus, it would be useful first to summarize

---

a college library at Oxford University in England. They had been held in the archives there since 1901, when they were unearthed in Egypt. Preliminary study has dated them to the middle of the first century A.D. ("Scraps Offer an Intriguing Clue on Jesus," *New York Times*, January 21, 1995, 11.)

9   John A. T. Robinson, Can *We Trust the New Testament?* (Grand Rapids: Eerdmans, 1977), 63.

briefly the chronology of the resurrection narrative. At dawn on resurrection Sunday there was an earthquake. An angel of the Lord came down and rolled away the stone from the sepulcher and sat on it. The soldiers, terrified, were transfixed for the moment and then returned to the city to tell their story and to be bribed by the priests and elders to report that the disciples had stolen the body. Then Mary Magdalene and the other women arrived to anoint Jesus. Finding the stone removed, they assumed that the body had been taken away by the Jews. Mary ran to find Peter and John and to tell them the situation. Meanwhile, the other women entered the tomb, and the angels told them of the resurrection and commanded them to tell the disciples. Soon Peter and John arrived at the tomb to confirm that the body was gone, and they soon left. Mary lingered behind weeping, and Jesus appeared to her first (Mark 16:9–11; John 20:11–18).

Mary Magdalene

Mary had gone with the other women to Joseph's garden to complete the anointing of Jesus' body. When the group saw that the tomb was open, Mary rushed away to tell the disciples (John 20:1–2), but the other women stayed at the tomb. John and Peter then ran to the tomb and found it empty. After they left, Mary returned. Consumed with sorrow, she met two angels who asked the reason for her weeping. As she explained her sorrow, and before they had a chance to announce the Resurrection, she became aware of someone (Jesus) standing behind her. The fact that she mistook him for a gardener is alone evidence for His truly physical nature. Her inability to recognize Him immediately was partly due to her emotional state and probably also to the degree of difference between His new and His old bodies. But He *spoke* to her and she responded, *clinging to Him.* Her *seeing* Him, *conversing* with Him, and *touching* Him demonstrates His corporeality. Then He commanded her to tell the disciples that He would ascend to the Father.

The Other Women

The other women (Matthew 28:1–10; Mark 16:1–8; Luke 24:1–11), including Mary the mother of James, and Salome, had remained in Joseph's garden while Mary Magdalene went off to get Peter and John. They entered the tomb and heard the angels declare that Jesus had risen from the dead. They received the instruction to tell the disciples to meet Him in Galilee. They then left the garden to convey the angelic message to the disciples, so when Mary returned to the tomb, they were no longer around. Soon after, Jesus met them too. They *saw* Him, *heard* Him repeat the angelic instruction, and *grasped* His feet in worship. They too had evidence of His *bodily* resurrection.

Peter

Jesus singled out Peter for a private interview at this juncture, as is clear from 1 Corinthians 15:5, Mark 16:7, and Luke 24:34. Although there is no record of what happened on this occasion, Jesus probably made an effort to restore him to fellowship and usefulness to the movement. Peter had already seen the empty tomb and no doubt had *seen* and *heard* the resurrected Christ; thus Jesus demonstrating that He was not just a spiritual being.

Two Disciples on the Way to Emmaus

Apparently on the afternoon of resurrection Sunday, Jesus met up with two disciples (Luke 24:13–35; Mark 16:12–13), Cleopas and his companion, on the way to Emmaus (the location of which is debated). He talked with them at length about messianic prophecy and its fulfillment. Finally, when they arrived at their home in Emmaus, He agreed to come in and have a meal with them, during the course of which He revealed Himself to them and then

127

disappeared. Thus, Jesus demonstrated His physical resurrection and reality by walking, speaking, and eating with
the pair.

Ten Disciples

Apparently later that evening Jesus simply appeared in
the midst of ten disciples (Luke 24:36–49; John 20:19–23),
where they were gathered in Jerusalem. Since He had
apparently just come through the walls, He frightened
them, and their first inclination was to believe that He was
only a spirit. But he quickly sought to persuade them
otherwise by showing them His hands and feet and side
(presumably the scars), inviting them to touch Him to
prove He had flesh and blood. Then to prove the reality of
His body further, He ate before them.

Eleven Disciples

Thomas was not present when the ten saw Jesus on
resurrection Sunday. When they told him what had happened, he responded in disbelief and declared that he
would not believe unless he could touch Jesus' scars. Jesus
responded to Thomas' doubts by appearing to the apostolic group again on the following Sunday when Thomas
was present (John 20:26–31). This time Thomas had his
wish and declared his faith in the risen Christ. Here's an
example of Jesus' patience with and special grace for the
doubters of our world who finally come to faith in Him.

The Seven at the Sea

On resurrection Sunday Jesus had told the disciples to
go back to Galilee. It was logical for them to do so because
their homes had been there, and apparently some of them
still had property there. The disciples remained in seclu-
sion for a couple of weeks after Passover and the excite-
ment of the Resurrection but then went north. One night,
seven of them went fishing on the Sea of Galilee, catching

almost nothing. Early in the morning, Jesus caught up with them and suggested that they cast their nets on the other side of the boat (for a miraculous catch), and then He had breakfast with them; as their host probably He ate also (John 21:1–14). The text says that this was the third time that He appeared to them after He was raised from the dead (v. 14). Again Jesus was visibly a human being as He met with the disciples; He talked with them and presumably ate with them. A second appearance to Peter (John 21:15–22) occurred at the time of the fishing expedition in Galilee. Jesus took Peter aside and engaged him in conversation about his love for the Master. Jesus asked Peter for a reaffirmation of his love three times—parallel to Peter's threefold denial before the Crucifixion.

Great Commission Appearance

The order of the Galilean appearances is not very clear. At some point Jesus met the disciples on a "mountain" (Matthew 28:16), perhaps a hillside such as the Mount of Beatitudes. There, as a very real human being and acting as the Potentate of Glory ("all authority is given unto me," Matthew 28:18), he gave them the Great Commission (Matthew 28:16–20; Mark 16:14–18); thus launching the world's greatest missionary society. "Go therefore and make disciples of all the nations, baptizing them in the name of the Father and the Son and the Holy Spirit, teaching them to observe all that I commanded you; and lo, I am with you always, even to the end of the age" (Matthew 28:19–20 NASB) were His orders.

Evidently also in Galilee, Jesus appeared to *five-hundred disciples* (1 Corinthians 15:6) and *James* (1 Corinthians 15:7). A large group of five hundred could meet in Galilee (where the number of followers was greater than in the south), out of reach of the Jewish authorities in Jerusalem. All of these people recognized Jesus as being very much alive and very human. They *saw* and *heard* Him.

Presumably James still lived in the Nazareth area. Although Jesus' brothers did not believe in Him while He was conducting His earthly ministry (John 7:5), James and Jude subsequently did. As part of the process of establishing James' faith, Jesus made a special appearance to him, and he became a leader in the Jerusalem church (Acts 15:13).

At the Ascension

At length, Jesus was ready to return to heaven (Acts 1:4–8). He gathered the disciples together on the Mount of Olives just east of Jerusalem. After presenting or showing Himself alive "by many convincing proofs, appearing to them over a period of forty days, and speaking of the things concerning the kingdom of God" (Acts 1:3 NASB), Jesus gave a command to wait for the Holy Spirit's special empowerment and then ascended to heaven. Jesus had made numerous previous appearances—possibly even more than those itemized above—meeting with people, talking with them, eating with them, showing them the scars of His crucifixion, and allowing them to touch Him. These appearances were not fleeting, fanciful, predictable, or conjured up but occurred at His pleasure to achieve the effect of convincing people of His resurrection. After the Ascension, the appearances abruptly stopped. He had *physically* returned to Heaven and *physical* appearances could no longer be expected.

Jesus' Appearance to Paul

Jesus' appearance to Paul (1 Corinthians 15:8) was a real physical appearance, on a par with the other physical appearances that he describes in 1 Corinthians 15 (see also Acts 9:1–9). Thus, Paul was qualified to be an apostle. He asserted in 1 Corinthians 9:1: "Am I not an apostle? Have I not seen Jesus our Lord? (NASB). Jesus appeared to Paul on the Damascus road, and this was the only time He appeared to an opponent. During the appearance, Jesus carried on a conversation with Paul and commanded him to go into the city of Damascus and await further instructions. "The conversion of Paul from his bitter hostility to the Christian movement in the beginning to his energetic defense of the gospel all around the Mediterranean world is further testimony to the resurrection."[10]

The Immediate Results of the Resurrection

Certainly the disciples, the faithful women, and Jesus' brothers were competent witnesses to the Resurrection. They would not have been fooled; they knew Him well.

An utter change in their demeanor immediately followed the Resurrection. No longer were they huddled in an upper room in Jerusalem "for fear of the Jews" (John 20:19 KJV). They became almost recklessly bold in their proclamation of the Resurrection and of the Gospel of the grace of God. Thrown into prison for preaching Christ and Him crucified and risen again, they immediately went back to preaching when released. Ordered to stop proclaiming the Gospel, they boldly declared, "We must obey God rather than men." Threatened with death for their activities, they said in effect, "So be it."

A change in the day of worship also followed the Resurrection. Devout Jews would be expected to observe the Sabbath as a day of worship and rest. Most of the converts to Christianity immediately after the Ascension were Jews, but soon they and their Gentile brothers and sisters in the faith began to worship on the first day of the week, in observation of the Resurrection. Indication of this change came by around A.D. 55, when in Troas (near Troy in northwest Asia Minor) Paul and others took Communion on the first day of the week (Acts 20:7). About the same time, Paul urged the Corinthians to set aside money on the first day

---

10 Clark H. Pinnock, *Set Forth Your Case* (Chicago: Moody Press, 1967), 98.

of the week for relief for the poor (1 Corinthians 16:2). Nearer the end of the century, when John was receiving the message of the Revelation, he spoke of being in the Spirit on the Lord's day (Revelation 1:10). Clearly the day of worship was changing as a result of resurrection observance and had nothing to do with some official action of Constantine in the fourth century, as "Seventh Dayists" assert. That is, Constantine did not change the Sabbath from Saturday to Sunday. The Sabbath continues to be Saturday, but Christians worship especially on Sunday in commemoration of the Resurrection and have done so from the earliest days of the church.

The pouring out of the Holy Spirit on the Day of Pentecost and the founding of the Christian church also result from the Resurrection. The apostle Peter in his famous sermon on the Day of Pentecost spoke of the Resurrection and the Ascension of Jesus as preconditions to the outpouring of the Spirit and the founding of the church (Acts 2:32–33). The power and ministry of the church in the world continues to witness to the resurrection of Jesus.

THE SIGNIFICANCE OF THE RESURRECTION

A study of the Resurrection would not be complete without some thoughts about its significance.

1. The Resurrection is a proof of Christ's person. He could hardly be reckoned as the God-man if He had remained in the grave.

2. The Resurrection is essential to our salvation. Were He to remain in the grave, He would have no more significance as the founder of our faith than would Mohammed or Buddha. The Resurrection marked a completed salvation; Romans 4:25 might better be translated, "who . . . was raised *on account of* our justification." There was no longer any need for Him to remain in the tomb; He had paid sin's penalty.

3. The Resurrection is essential to Christ's present work of intercession (Hebrews 7:25), advocacy (1 John 2:1), and preparing a place for us (John 14:2–3).

4. The Resurrection is essential to His future work of the resurrection of humanity, His judgments, and His reign on David's throne. Paul views the resurrection of Christ as the firstfruits of those who had died (1 Corinthians 15:20). That is, His resurrection is the firstfruits and the basis of the resurrection of all humanity who are linked to Him by faith. His bodily resurrection guarantees ours also.

5. The Resurrection is evidence of the inspiration of Scripture. The Resurrection is the fulfillment of many prophecies and as such gives support to the whole doctrine of inspiration.

6. Jesus' last appearance was connected with our mission. In a sense, His mission was accomplished. He wants us to take up where He left off, so He has left us with the Great Commission: "Go therefore and make disciples of all the nations" (Matthew 28:19 NASB).

Can I believe in the resurrection of Jesus? The evidences for it are extensive and powerful. Civilization would not make much sense without it. How do I really know that Jesus is alive today? The believer can say, "I talked with Him five minutes ago.

Chapter 7

CAN I REALLY BELIEVE THAT GOD EXISTS?

Rationalism, at least the form of rationalism that denies the existence of God or the gods, could be dangerous to one's health, or to the health of the state in ancient times. To be more specific, the ancient Greek city-states linked the worship of their particular patron deity and loyalty to the state. Religion became a prop of the state and furnished some of the thread that helped to hold the social fabric together. One who denied the existence of the gods of the state became a public enemy; guilty of treason, and for treason they could be executed. As an example in point, the philosopher Socrates (c. 469–399 B.C.), charged with "impiety" to the gods of Athens, was forced to drink hemlock as capital punishment because of his questioning.

Later when orthodox Christianity became the universal faith of the West, there was no real fear that atheism would upset the body politic. And when philosophy, especially that of Aristotle, reappeared in strength in the medieval university during the twelfth and thirteenth centuries, Scholastics such as Thomas Aquinas (1225-74) sought to use philosophy, or rational argument, as a "handmaiden" or support for theology. Thus, Aquinas worked out his well-known arguments for the existence of God. And these have continued to exercise an appeal in modern times, even after the decline of Scholasticism and the rise of the Enlightenment and modern rationalism.

AQUINAS' ARGUMENTS FOR THE EXISTENCE OF GOD

A brief statement of Aquinas' arguments serves as a good beginning for any discussion of how we know that God exists. Aquinas held that the existence of God is not something we can know directly. It is not a given, as the color of this book is a given. Nor is it known or discovered by intuition or direct insight but is inferred or deduced; it rests on argument—on reasoning from a given to something inferred. These arguments appear in the first part of volume one of his *Summa Theologica*. Aquinas presents five arguments.[1]

1. Argument from change or motion. Aquinas points out the obvious: the fact of change or motion in nature; things are constantly in flux. Behind every instance of change or motion is a prior case of change or motion. Arguing back through the process of change or motion, we arrive at an Unmoved Mover, or Prime Mover, or Unchanging One—put in motion by no other. This One, we call God.

2. Argument from causation. The argument from causation is similar to the previous one. We are faced everywhere with the fact of the cause-effect relationship. A given effect is caused by something. Arguing back through the process. we come to the point where we must believe in a First Cause, Itself uncaused. Again he insists that this One we call God.

3. Argument from contingency. In nature every object and event is contingent on another. Aquinas argues from

---

1 One of the more easily accessible summaries of Thomas Aquinas' work is Etienne Gilson, *The Philosophy of St. Thomas Aquinas,* ed. by G. A. Erlington (New York: Dorset, n. d.). See especially chapters 4 and 5 for the arguments for the existence of God.

contingency back to a Necessary Being, contingent on nothing or no one. This he calls God.

4. Argument from degrees of excellence. Some things are more-or-less good, true, or more noble than others. We then talk about something that is best, truest, or noblest. The notion of degrees of excellence implies the notion of perfection. He argues back to that One who is perfection and the cause of all goodness and every other perfection.

5. Argument from harmony or design. Nature functions together in a workable pattern. The winds, the tides, the heavier fur coat on an animal in a cold climate, and the perfect functioning together of the organs of the body are examples of an infinite list of adaptation or accord in nature. From this Aquinas argues to an intelligent Being who ordains or manages all this. This Being, we call God. If He is the great Designer and if He makes things work as they do, He must be provident or involved in the affairs of the solar system and certainly of earth. If He is involved and makes things go as they do, He must be omnipotent, or all powerful, and omnipresent, or everywhere present.

Eventually in his theological system, St. Thomas faces the problem of evil, declaring that the problem arises in the free will of humanity—the ability to choose between good and evil. His will must be free in some sense or some degree or he is not responsible for his acts and should not be rewarded or punished for them. Moreover, he declares that God made human beings rational and being rational includes having freedom of mind and will.

THE RELIGIOUS "WAGER" OF PASCAL

A later scholar who has been widely influential in his comments on the existence of God is Blaise Pascal (1623–62). While Thomas Aquinas wrote in an age of Christian faith, Pascal wrote in a day when the new science of Copernicus and Galileo and the new philosophy of Descartes and Hobbes had helped to create an age of unbelief and indifference. To such an age Pascal, one of the outstanding physicists and mathematicians of his time, was busy addressing an apology for the Christian faith when he died. He did not finish the book, and what existed came to be known in French as *Pensées*, or in English as *Thoughts*.

Pascal differed with Aquinas in that he did not believe that man, by the use of his reason, could argue the existence of God from the existence of nature. He said that some individuals are too skeptical or indifferent in matters of religious belief, and no appeal to reason or to natural theology will dissolve their doubts, denials, or indifference. This is true because they are too hardened and because human reason is unequal to producing a rational theology.

If one cannot be brought to a knowledge of God by reason, how then can it happen? Pascal's answer is: through his emotions. His famous aphorism is that "the heart hath its reasons, which the reason knows not of." The best that reason can do is present and defend what Pascal calls a "wager" or a bet that God exists. Individuals must see for themselves that their happiness lies in belief in and love of God. When they have discovered that fact, their skepticism and indifference will be replaced by faith and happiness. Pascal himself had a life-changing mystical experience on November 23, 1654.

The essence of his argument is this. The strongest proof for the existence of God is the need felt by the soul for the sustaining presence of such a Being in an otherwise empty universe. Man, of himself, is ignorant, helpless, and alone. In his quest for happiness and goodness, he is confronted by an alien, indifferent, even hostile world. So "Man finds his lasting happiness only in God." He said, "Our ultimate good is to know Him certainly."

He is satisfied to argue from our need for God to the existence of God. But he does not ask his reader to follow him in that jump. Instead he proposes a wager. "If you wager that He does exist, and He does, you gain all; if you wager that He does, and He does not, you lose nothing. . . . Wager then, unhesitatingly, that He does exist. . . . Now, what will happen to you if you take this side in the religious wager? I tell you that you will gain this life . . . You will know at last you have wagered on a certainty, an infinity, for which you have risked nothing." And as a result of your taking this side in the religious wager, "You will be trustworthy, honorable, humble, grateful, generous, friendly, sincere, and true."[2]

THE WORK OF RICHARD SWINBURNE

One of the most ambitious recent efforts to evaluate the arguments for the existence of God from an almost purely philosophical standpoint is that of Richard Swinburne, Nolloth Professor of Philosophy of the Christian Religion at Oxford. His *The Existence of God* was first published in 1979, but the revised edition came out in 1992 (Oxford).[3] Although in the nature of the case he has to consider each argument separately, he does not allow them to stand as separately as does Thomas Aquinas but tries to discover the total effect of all the arguments taken together. In addition to the those in Aquinas' list, he adds discussion of arguments from morality, providence, history, miracles, and religious experience. In the main part of the text, he maintains that the argument from contingency (otherwise known as the cosmological argument) and the argument from design (also known as the teleological argument) are somewhat weak. But he gives some credence to arguments from religious experience, history, and miracles. In the argument from history and miracle he deals with the occurrence of events in history that seem to be naturally

---

2 Quoted in Alburey Castell, *An Introduction to Modern Philosophy* (New York: Macmillan, 1946), 36–37.

3 Richard Swinburne, *The Existence of God*, rev. ed. (Oxford: Oxford University Press, 1992).

inexplicable and therefore to some degree confirm theism. His argument from religious experience appears more in detail in the next chapter.

Swinburne fully admits that the "only plausible alternative to theism" is a view that the world has "no explanation," and he does not find that appealing as a "probable alternative."[4] He states that theism has a "remarkable ability to make sense" of an otherwise puzzling world[5] and concludes that it is easier to defend the concept of an infinite God than of One who is limited in some way.[6] Then, he concludes that religious experience, taken together with nature and history, show it "to be quite likely" that there is a God who created and sustains the universe.[7] In an appendix added in 1992 he further discusses the argument from design (called the "Fine-Tuning of the Universe") and now states that it is "strong confirming evidence of the existence of God."[8]

THE MORAL ARGUMENT OF C. S. LEWIS

C. S. Lewis seeks to lead persons to a belief in God through the moral argument. His mental exercises appear in Mere *Christianity*,[9] and the development of his thought runs something like this. As we interact with other people, we have a sense of fair play, or decent behavior, or a standard of what is right and wrong. There is a so-called Law of Nature or decent behavior to which all people subscribe. Individuals may disobey the Law of Nature, and in fact none of us really keeps the law. Even when we break this law we expect others to keep it. The moral law is not

---

4 Ibid., 287.

5 Ibid., 289.

6 Ibid., 282–83.

7 Ibid., 291.

8 Ibid., 322.

9 C. S. Lewis, *Mere Christianity,* rev. ed. (New York: Macmillan, 1952).

merely an instinct; it may be called on to encourage or suppress instinct. For example, fighting is an instinct that commonly needs to be suppressed to prevent our being quarrelsome, but in a soldier fighting needs to be encouraged. Morality is not merely social convention either, for we tend to judge national or individual moralities against a perceived standard of right and wrong.

As we live life, we come to recognize that beyond human behavior is a real law that none of us made and that constantly presses in on us. What lies behind this law is more like a mind than is anything else we know. It is conscious, a power that makes it what it is. As human beings, we find ourselves under a moral law that we neither made nor can forget and that we know we ought to obey. We don't exist on our own but are under a law that somebody or something—a Power, a Director, a Guide—wants us to observe in a certain way. This moral law is very demanding. In fact, we would not want a Power (God?) that did not detest our human greed and exploitation. If it did not it would not be good. So, this Power becomes the supreme terror and we now need a grace to save us from the terror of God. Thus, Lewis argues to the existence of God who sets and embodies the moral standard of the universe and then proceeds to describe how the terror of God is handled by the grace of God in Christ.

THE CONTRIBUTION OF MORTIMER ADLER

The immensely popular author, Mortimer J. Adler undertook in his book *How to Think About God*[10] to discover what reasons there were, if any, for affirming that God exists. Not a Christian, he came through philosophical

---

10 Mortimer J. Adler, *How to Think About God* (New York: Macmillan, 1980). Adler is author of forty-seven books, chairman of the Board of Editors of the Encyclopedia Britannica, and Director of the Institute of Philosophical Research.

inquiry to believe that the best traditional argument for the existence of God is the cosmological argument, or preferably the argument from contingency. The very heavily philosophical line of argument that Adler follows involves, among other things, first a demonstration that the parts of the cosmos are dependent on or contingent on the cosmos. They come into existence and pass away, but they do not come into existence out of nothingness nor cease to exist in a reduction to nothingness.

But then what about the contingency of the cosmos as a whole? He answers that the cosmos that exists is one of many possible universes and, in fact, it might not have existed at all. But here it is and what keeps it from being reduced to nothing is contingent on an uncaused cause. The cosmos "needs an efficient cause of its continuing existence."[11] Then, if there is an efficient cause to keep the cosmos going, it will thereby also sustain the operation or existence of all the individual things that are its parts.[12] Moreover, if one can account for a power to keep the cosmos going, it is possible to argue to the institution of the laws and processes that set the cosmos going in the first place. So, a superior being as creator is affirmed beyond a reasonable doubt.[13] He is willing to go on record as having "reasonable grounds for affirming God's existence."[14] And Adler concludes by arguing that if God is the Supreme Being, He must be omnipotent, omniscient, supremely intelligent, and one who wills.[15] Adler must have done a good job of arguing himself into a theistic position because after writing this book he made a Christian profession of faith and was baptized.

---

11 Ibid., 149.

12 Ibid., 147.

13 Ibid., 150.

14 Ibid., 150.

15 Ibid., 160–61.

THE EFFECT OF THE TRAGIC CIRCUMSTANCES OF LIFE

What might lead an atheist or an agnostic to believe in the existence of God. Naturally the answer is slightly different in the case of each one of those that have become Christians. But there is a recurring refrain. Often the circumstances of life have become so bitter, life has become so futile that they have come to the end of themselves. In the words of a leading Canadian evangelical of the last generation, they have been "crowded to Christ." Or in the words of the book of Ecclesiastes, as they look out over life, they declare that "all is vanity" (Ecclesiastes 1:2).

In the dire circumstances of life, some try God. A typical example comes from the experience of a young father I once knew. He had been living without God in a rather self-confident manner. Then his son fell ill, and all that could be done for the boy was not enough. For once the young man felt helpless. His physical strength, brains, and money could not meet the current need. As he looked at his situation, his first comment on his way to faith was, "It makes you stop and think."

A more dramatic example of an theist who found his way to God comes from the family of the nation's best-known atheist, Madalyn Murray O'Hair. Mrs. O'Hair was the one who used the school experience of her grade–school-age son, William J. Murray, to persuade the Supreme Court in 1963 to ban prayer and Bible reading from the public schools. In *My Life without God*, Murray chronicled his terrible life up to his conversion to Christ in 1980 at age thirty-three. Near the end of the odyssey he made three very revealing comments. As he longed for revenge against some of the evils that had befallen him, he said, "I knew there had to be some retribution in the universe."[16] There

---

16 William J. Murray, *My Life without God* (Nashville: Thomas Nelson, 1982), 231.

was sense of a power in the universe that would judge evil. Then, as he met evil person, one day he came to the conclusion: "There has to be a God because there certainly is a devil. I have met him, talked to him, and touched him. He is the personification of evil. He is Tom Evans, my mother, and others like them I have known."[17] And finally he decided, "There had to be good, because I had looked into the eyes of evil. There had to be a God, because I had held hands with the devil."[18] Somehow his overwhelming sense of the evil in persons he had known, the evil experiences he had been through, his own short-comings, and the futility of life had convinced him that there had to be a God. He learned to trust God too in overcoming his alcoholism.

THE PROBLEM OF A WORLD
SEEMINGLY OUT OF CONTROL

There are, of course, all sorts of things that keep people from believing in God in general or the God of the Bible in particular. We often hear the comment that if there is a God in Heaven, or if the course of history is under the control of God, why does He not do something about the mess we are in? Why does He not intervene to end war, racial injustice, economic injustice, inequality in general, and the major tragedies that descend on humanity with increasing regularity? How is it that so often evil seems to triumph and both the good and good people seem to suffer? Why do bad things happen to good people? Of course the answer is long and would fill a book or a whole set of books, but there are brief suggestions that will help to clear the air.

1. God has granted humanity a will that is free, within divine limitations, to act in history. Unfortunately, we all have corrupted natures; we contaminate all we touch.

---

17 Ibid., 232–233.
18 Ibid., 237.

Scripture is quite pointed: "There is none righteous, no, not one" (Romans 3:10 KJV); "There is none that doeth good, no, not one" (Romans 3:12 KJV). These statements do not mean that we never choose to do good but rather indicate that we are not basically good. We are sinful creatures who sometimes misrepresent, take unfair advantage of others, let greed get the better of us, or stomp on others in the rush to get ahead. And in self-gratification we choose to do things that are very self destructive or destructive of others.

We choose to do a lot of things that have built-in catastrophic results and we know it. Literature of all kinds reports on the health risks connected with smoking. Every day we hear reports of terrible accidents occurring because people choose to drink and drive. We know that birth defects result when women choose to drink or smoke or use drugs during pregnancy. Because people choose a drug-induced momentary high, we have a plague that destroys individuals, families, and communities and burdens governmental budgets at all levels. Premarital sex, extramarital sex, commercial sex, and recreational sex have, along with drug abuse, brought on a worldwide AIDS epidemic, or at least have contributed to high incidences of venereal disease. The middle-age population of whole villages in the AIDS belt in Africa has been virtually killed off and grandparents are left to care for grandchildren, many of whom are infected. This results almost exclusively from a choice to engage in recreational and commercial sex. In the latter case, prostitutes are heavily infected with the HIV virus. Currently, the AIDS epidemic is raging in Southeast Asia, especially because of commercial sex.

All of the trouble and suffering hinted at in these last few sentences is a result of the deliberate lifestyle choices of free individuals. Religiously oriented individuals often construct statements about God's judgment on the sins of drinking, smoking, drug abuse, and premarital or extramarital sex, but none of that is necessary. It is enough to point out to biblically uninformed people that all of the above involves human choice to engage in acts that have *built in* destructive effects and incur high risk. Society need not blame God for its sins.

2. God will intervene some day and will right the wrongs of our world; He will punish evil doers. But in grace He postpones judgment to give human beings additional opportunities for repentance. The truth is that God is "not willing that any should perish, but that all should come to repentance" (2 Peter 3:9 KJV). While we need to be careful about omniscience or dogmatism in such matters, we may at least timidly suggest that some tragedies in our world (especially those occurring in countries largely closed to the Gospel) have resulted in many individuals coming to a knowledge of Christ and may have occurred in part for that reason. This has been true, for example, among Iranians fleeing from the Islamic Revolution in Iran, among those displaced because of the Gulf War, among refugees from Afghanistan, among individuals uprooted by drought and war in West Africa, and among those caught in the terrible civil war in Sudan. In the latter case, one of the most significant revivals in the world has resulted.

3. The world at large does not want God to interfere in their affairs. Even a large percentage of evangelical Christians really are not interested in doing God's will—marching to God's drumbeat on a daily basis. God takes them at their word and lets them alone; He lets them stew in their own juice, so to speak. In answer to the question of why God lets this or that happen or why does He not do something about this or that, we might reply, "Have you ever asked Him to do something about it?" Or, "Do you really want Him to take over and direct a solution?" An honest answer would be, "No."

4. Apparently there is a degree of divine judgment that people suffer for their sin in this life (interim or proximate

justice) in addition to punishment that awaits in the life beyond (eternal justice). The Old Testament prophets made it clear that Israel of old suffered because of economic and social injustice in the body politic and that both Israel and Judah would go into captivity because of their idolatry and other failures. And while Christians will someday stand before the judgment seat of Christ, there is apparently some interim justice for them too. For example, Paul told the Corinthians that for their sin "many are weak and sickly among you, and many sleep" (had died prematurely, 1 Corinthians 11:30 KJV). Evidently interim judgment is sometimes remedial.

5. In the counsels of divine justice, there seems to be a quota of iniquity that is allowed a people before it is punished either in a minor way or by obliteration. And it seems that God will deal with a nation when it has reached such a place. This is not pure speculation. In Genesis 15 God was having a conversation with Abraham that concerned His promise to give Palestine to Abraham's descendants in perpetuity. In the process, He said that the promise did not mean that the Hebrews would always inhabit the land. In fact, they would be out of the Land and held in bondage in a strange land (Egypt) for four-hundred years (v. 13). Finally, at the end of that time, the Hebrews would return to Palestine, "for the sin of the Amorites has not yet reached its full measure" (v. 16 NIV). After the four-hundred years of bondage in Egypt, the Hebrews left in the Exodus and entered Canaan. Then, God commanded them to exterminate the Amorites (Deuteronomy 20:17). Evidently by that time the sin of the Amorites had reached "full measure."

What God is saying here is that He is in control of the course of history. He will watch over the Hebrews and He will judge the sin of the nations when they are "ripe for punishment" (Genesis 15:16, Revised English Bible). We may wonder out loud whether Sodom and Gomorrah had reached their quota of iniquity when destroyed by divine judgment (Genesis 19), or whether Pompeii and the other cities at the foot of Mount Vesuvius had reached that point in A.D. 79. When we learn from the excavations about the degree to which Pompeii was given over to sexual preoccupation, for example (even in the motifs on furniture and lamps), we may conclude that life in the city was very base. We may also wonder about the iniquity quotas of modern cities and countries.

6. There is also the question of why bad things happen to good people, and whether there is indeed a God in Heaven who is fair and just. This is not a book on theology, and of course we cannot discuss the question of how good one should be to merit escaping a host of tragedies. As human beings all of us are in the flow of life and cannot escape the effects of earthquakes, hurricanes, attacks in wartime, air and water pollution (with their cancer causing agents), and much more.

When it comes to avowed believers, there should be an expectation of trouble. Jesus warned that as the world hated Him, it would hate those who follow Him (John 15:18). Moreover, the devil as a roaring lion stalks believers, seeking whom he may devour (1 Peter 5:8). The first two chapters of Job are especially instructive. Satan still has access to God and does what he can to make life miserable for believers as well as destroy their witness in the world. And finally, God is in the business of conforming believers to the image of His Son. People often quote Romans 8:28, "all things work together for good," when consoling friends. But they divorce Romans 8:28 from verse 29. In the latter it becomes clear that many of the difficulties of life (v. 28) work together for the good of conforming us to the image of His Son (v. 29). They may act as a kind of sandpaper to take off the rough edges.

Can I believe that God exists? Secular and Christian philosophers have mounted significant arguments for the existence of God. And on further investigation, questions about whether God is really in control of our disheveled world tend to melt away. Of course the arguments of this chapter have to stand alongside those of the rest of the book. Arguments from natural revelation, from nature, and from philosophy, can take us only so far. They must be supplemented by an inspired Bible that can give us more detail about God and make the case stronger (chapter 2). And we really cannot know and believe in this God of the universe without the divine invasion, the coming of the divine Jesus to tell us about this God and make Him personal to us (*see* chapters 4 and 5). On a personal level, as I walk and talk with Him day by day, I shall really come to know that God exists.

Chapter 8

CAN I DRAW SOME ASSURANCE OF THE CHRISTIAN FAITH FROM EXPERIENCE?

"**T**he proof of the pudding is in the eating"[1] is a well-known adage that helps to describe an important apologetic for Christianity. A great many who have responded to the invitation to "taste and see that the LORD is good" (Psalm 34:8 KJV) will testify that God does indeed exist and the Christian faith is real, effective, and sufficient for the challenges of life. But then the question arises as to whether they are deluded or whether they have merely achieved some psychological reorientation that now enables them to cope more effectively. Let's explore the question.

---

1   Often quoted, it comes from Cervantes' *Don Quixote*, part 1, book 4 (A.D.1605).

CONVERSIONS WITH SUPERNATURAL EFFECTS

To begin with, a great many conversions have been accompanied by supernatural effects. So striking are the changes that those familiar with the individuals involved are impressed by what God has done. The greatest single recounting of such dramatic conversions has appeared on *Unshackled*, the weekly broadcast of the Pacific Garden Mission of Chicago. The theme or principle behind the broadcast is, "Christ can break the fetters of sin and set the sinner free." The broadcast began in 1950 on WGN, Chicago, moving in 1957 to WLS and in 1960 to WCFL (also in Chicago). Since the late 1960s, when the secular stations were no longer willing to carry religious broadcasts of this type, the program has been aired over WMBI (the radio voice of the Moody Bible Institute) and its affiliates and contracting stations.

During these forty-five years of broadcasting, *Unshackled* has dramatized countless conversions. Particularly impressive are the numerous cases of alcoholism, on which the medical profession had given up or for which there seemed to be no cure. Because of its location and the type of work the mission does, it has especially ministered to alcoholics. Many are the instances of "incurables," who have been able to quit "cold turkey" soon after conversion. An example of these dramatic changes occurred in the life of Jack Odell, for many years director of *Unshackled*. After conversion he continued to struggle with his habit, with no success. Finally one night as he gave his testimony at the Pacific Garden Mission, he sensed a sudden and complete release from his habit (disease).[2]

Of course there have been drug addicts, compulsive gamblers, and all sorts of other "shackled" or "bound"

---

2   James R. Adair, *The Old Lighthouse* (Chicago: Moody Press, 1966), 143.

individuals whose release has been chronicled on the broadcast. Remarkable stories of these and other rehabilitations have surfaced all over the world since the beginning of the church, and they constitute a powerful witness to the truth of the Gospel. Because of the countless numbers of persons who have been rehabilitated, not all could not be merely the product of some psychological adjustment or improvement.

CONVERSIONS BRING PEACE, COMFORT, AND THE STRENGTH TO COPE

Obviously most conversions do not involve such drastic or public evidence of the validity of Christianity. The Christian faith possesses the power of making over the lives of people—putting them at peace with themselves, God, and others; helping to rehabilitate their personalities; giving them comfort and stability in the midst of trial; instilling a love for others (believers and nonbelievers); and enabling them to cope more effectively with life in general. Whatever others may say about God's existence or the reality of the faith, day-by-day experience with God is for Christians an apologetic or evidence of the truth of the faith described in the Bible. As Ramm has stated, "Christianity verifies itself in meeting the deepest needs of the human heart."[3]

CHRISTIAN CONVERSION AND MINISTRY EXPLAINED BY PSYCHOLOGY

There are those who try to explain away Christian conversion, describing it as a result of some psychological reorientation. Further, they argue that the success of evangelists in public campaigns, whether a Jonathan Edwards, a Whitefield, a Wesley, or a contemporary evangelist, re-

---

3 Bernard Ramm, *Protestant Christian Evidences* (Chicago: Moody Press, 1953), 214.

sults from a play on the emotions or an ability to manipulate people. There is no question about the effect of psychology or the psychological approach in contemporary evangelism. For example, note that the invitation hymn, "Just As I Am" In its five verses, it has the congregation singing, "I come," ten times in unison. In Fanny Crosby's gospel song, "Jesus Is Calling," the words *calling today* or *come* appear seventeen times. This unanimous appeal *is* psychologically suggestive. Many respond to the appeal; but after an evangelistic service is over, many who have responded to a public invitation melt away and are never heard from again. A minister of a large evangelistic church once said to me, "I do well to hold two out of ten who respond to a public invitation." There is no way of knowing whether his experience is typical, but it does point out the danger of equating mass or even individual response to the Gospel with true expression of faith in Christ.

But with this warning about conversion, are we willing to dismiss the whole Christian venture as a product of psychology or psychological manipulation? Is the evangelical Christian life to be equated with that of the New Age and its use of est (Ehrhardt Seminar Training) or Forum, in which brainwashing techniques of physical exhaustion, inducing fear, guilt, inadequacy, hopelessness, and the crowd effect occur? Not at all.

To be sure, some evangelists have gone down the road of emotional manipulation, but a great many have not. Jonathan Edwards, often accused by uninformed people of playing on the emotions, was actually scared to death of emotion in his services. Customarily he read his sermons, and in an effort to avoid emotion further, assumed an unemotional stance, fixing his eye on the bell rope in the back of the church while preaching. Whitefield, often but not always somewhat emotional, opened the door to the charge of emotionalism with his extemporaneous preaching and his belief that preaching should not be dull. John

Wesley was not necessarily emotional but put a lot of emphasis on personal experience, personal conduct, and a call to holiness. Preaching that concentrates in some detail on personal conduct and how to change it does, in the nature of the case, frequently stir the emotions. John White, evangelical psychiatrist, has dealt sensitively with the relation of psychology and the moving of the Holy Spirit in *When the Spirit Comes With Power* (InterVarsity Press, 1988), showing that sometimes emotional expression in church work is the result of a sovereign working of the Holy Spirit. Parenthetically, it may be useful to note that in the earlier history of the church down through the Great Awakening and the Second Evangelical Awakening, there were no public invitations in a mass-evangelistic approach. That began with Charles G. Finney early in the nineteenth century.

Earlier in this chapter we noted that many who are converted are released from various kinds of addiction or bondage that requires something far beyond a mere psychological reorientation. Moreover, we all hear of cases of physical healing or surgical success that go beyond the ability of the medical profession. In fact, doctors and nurses sometimes attest to the miraculous. In my own experience, when I was quite young, a neighbor lady went to the hospital for surgery. When the doctor opened her up, he saw evidence of massive cancer. Declaring further surgery to be useless, he closed the incision and sent her home. She sent an urgent letter for prayer to my pastor, who at that time conducted a radio broadcast. Soon she was completely healed, and she died many years later of some other problem. Such unexplained cases give evidence of a Higher Power who is involved in human affairs.

And when it comes to prayer, there is plenty of evidence that it is not merely some psychological reorientation or subconscious exercise, with no power outside the individual. Two examples will suffice. George Müller (1805–98), born in Prussia, went to England in 1829 for missionary training. There, he eventually joined the Plymouth Brethren and in 1835 felt led to found an orphanage in Bristol, supported entirely on faith. He operated on the principle that there should be no appeals to human agencies for support, only prayer to God. One annual report would be published for the encouragement of God's people and to assure honest accountability in finances. Life was hard in the early days. Over forty times in two consecutive years the supervisors began the day without the means to buy food, but food was always provided. Müller's work grew until there were two-thousand orphans in five large houses. The institution continued on exactly the same principles all during his lifetime, without lack, and his example prompted the establishment of orphanages based on similar faith principles in many lands. Obviously, no amount of psychological remodeling or mental telepathy could account for the supply of Müller's material needs; the Holy Spirit had to lay it on the hearts of God's people to provide for the needs of the orphanage.

An even more remarkable example of supernatural provision appears in the work of the Door of Hope Mission in Shanghai, China. At the beginning of World War II, there were over two-thousand children in the mission orphanage. As hostilities developed, all American, British and other Western European mission personnel had to leave the work. Moreover, all funds from the West were cut off. In addition, the Christian community in China was in no position to offer much help. The leadership was forced to depend entirely on God to supply all needs—usually from secular sources. As they faced the need for soap, rice, or whatever else ran low, the leadership and the children fell to their knees before God, and He always remarkably supplied—all through the war. Obviously the provision was supernatural. There could have been no human manipulation of supply sources.

THE ARGUMENT FOR RELIGIOUS
PERCEPTUAL CLAIMS

In the last chapter on the arguments for the existence of God, we made reference to the work of Richard Swinburne.[4] Now we look more fully at his argument from religious experience. As he develops his thesis, he suggests that if there is a God, we would expect Him to show Himself to or speak to some individuals capable of worshiping Him. The argument from religious experience holds that this revelation has in fact occurred and many have experienced God.

Swinburne's thought process goes like this: Individuals claim to perceive God or to be aware of Him. One has an experience of God if this perception is indeed caused by God's being present. There are public and private perceptions of God, and most of the time the perception is private. Swinburne identifies five kinds of religious experience. In the first, the individual experiences the supernatural by perceiving a nonreligious object; e. g., something in nature, such as a sunset, reminds one of God's handiwork. The second involves experiences of unusual public objects; e. g., the appearance of the risen Jesus to the disciples as described in Luke 24:36–49, where He looked and talked like Jesus. In the third category one has a private experience communicated by normal vocabulary; e. g., Joseph's dream in Matthew 1:20–24. In the fourth kind of experience, the individual has certain private sensations that cannot be described by normal vocabulary. And in the fifth, there is only a vague awareness of God without experiencing specific sensations.

Next Swinburne introduces the principle of credulity: that the way "things seem to be is good grounds for a belief

---

4 Richard Swinburne, *The Existence of God,* rev. ed. (Oxford: Oxford University Press, 1992).

about how things are."[5] As he observes, there are considerations ("good grounds") that defeat some perceptual claims. It may be shown on one basis or another that the individual's word cannot be trusted. Or it may be demonstrated that claims of this type have been proven false in the past. Sometimes, too, the claim is so extreme that it needs corroboration before it becomes probable. Or some may possibly account for the experience on other than supernatural bases.

But having said this, Swinburne observes that, on the principle of testimony, we ordinarily believe that what people tell us they have experienced or perceived, happened. This is especially true if there are no solid grounds for believing something to the contrary. We grow up accepting this basic principle, and religious perceptual claims ought to be taken as seriously as those of any other kind.[6] Moreover, one's religious experience can be backed up by the testimony of countless others. And even those who have had no experience of, or with, God will still see some evidence for the existence of God and His operation among humanity on the basis of the testimony of the many who have had such experiences. So, in conclusion, he points to the "considerable evidential force of religious experience," based on the principle "that apparent perceptions ought to be taken at their face value in the absence of positive reason for challenge."[7]

IMPACT OF CHRISTIANITY IN THE WORLD

Evidence that "the proof of the pudding is in the eating," when it comes to Christianity, is abundant even from a brief look at its impact in the world. On the mission fields, during revival times, and in great social movements, Christianity

---

5   Ibid., 254.

6   Ibid., 276.

7   Ibid., 275.

has significantly influenced the betterment of individuals and the remaking of society.

On the Mission Fields

On the mission fields of the world where Christian standards have not radically influenced social structure or family relationships, the power of Christianity is especially evident. The contrast between the lives of Christians and non-Christians is marked. As Hamilton observes,

> When a dissipated and dissolute scoundrel, who treats his wife and children as so many head of cattle, changes into a kind father and loving husband, who discards his sinful habits and seeks to spend his days winning others to Christ, we know that a power has been at work in the heart of such a one entirely different from natural causes. Christianity works![8]

On the whole, however, missionaries have not concentrated on eliminating polygamy or in other ways trying to restructure society. Commonly they could not do so because colonial or local powers stood in their way. But the missionaries were free to develop educational systems that would produce an educated laity and clergy and in other ways improve the lives of the people. Moreover, missionaries have constructed medical facilities to meet their physical needs. In many places in the world, missionaries have been almost solely responsible for beginnings in both of these fields, even though governments may have subsequently built extensively on those foundations. In any case, much social advancement can be traced to the evangelical effort.

---

8 Floyd E. Hamilson, *Basis of Christian Faith*, 3d ed. (New York: Harper, 1946), 321.

During Revival Times

During revival times individuals have a heightened awareness of God and a heightened experience with Him—certainly an increased belief in God and His involvement with human beings. There are now scores of thousands of accounts by and about individuals involved in the Great Awakening of the eighteenth century,[9] the Second Evangelical Awakening (cf. about 1800), the Finney revivals, the Revival of 1858, the Moody revivals, the Revival of 1905, and more. It would be futile to try to capture the spirit of those revivals here, when whole sets of books could be filled with the accounts. Probably the greatest historian of revivals worldwide is J. Edwin Orr. A partial list of his publications includes, *The Eager Feet* (Second Evangelical Awakening); *The Second Evangelical Awakeninq in Britain; The Fervent Prayer* (revival of 1858); and *The Flaming Tongue* (early twentieth-century revivals). The constant inference and assumption is that as these revived individuals had an experience with God, their lives were changed, and they changed their communities for the better. This is certainly the testimony of contemporary writers. And, of course, improvement in society helps to give evidence for the existence of God and His working in the world. Furthermore, the overwhelming power of God as it came down on numerous congregations, with the resultant public outcry for mercy and salvation, is experiential evidence for God's existence and the reality of the Christian faith.

A typical comment on social betterment is that of David Rice, speaking at the Presbyterian Synod of Kentucky in

---

9 Among the useful literature on the Great Awakening are Edwin S. Gaustad, *The Great Awakening in New England*; Wesley M. Gewehr, *The Great Awakening in Virginia*; Charles H. Maxson, *The Great Awakening in the Middle Colonies*; and Howard F. Vos, *The Great Awakening in Connecticut* (Ph.D. diss., Northwestern University).

1803: "some neighborhoods, noted for their vicious and profligate manners are now much noted for their piety and good order. Drunkards, profane swearers, liars, quarrelsome persons etc., are remarkably reformed."[10] The Second Evangelical Awakening (c. 1800, the time during which this comment was made) usually gets credit for accomplishing a reformation of the frontier, especially in Kentucky and Tennessee.

Although we have numerous tempting comments of moral reform during revival from various places in the world, there is not, to my knowledge, a statistical study of a region that tabulates crime for a period before, during, and after a great revival, to see what kind of an impact revival really made—what sort of apologetic Christian experience can really provide. During my own extensive study of the Great Awakening in Connecticut, I was not able to make such a tabulation either, because the county court records were at the time boxed and being moved to a new facility and were therefore inaccessible. A useful book on the impact of revival on American life during the nineteenth century is Timothy L. Smith's, *Revivalism and Social Reform.*

Closely related to some of these revival movements were great hymn and gospel song writers. Certainly the experience that such individuals had with God is more intense and more insightful than that of most of the rest of us. Charles Wesley (1707–88), with his hymns, helped make possible the evangelistic success of his brother John. He is variously credited with the composition of 7,200 or 6,500 hymns. Among his best known compositions are, "Love Divine," "And Can It Be." "O For a Thousand Tongues," and "Hark! the Herald Angels Sing." Somewhat contemporary with the Wesleys, but not part of their move-

---

10 Catherine C. Cleveland, *The Great Revival in the West,* 1797–1805 (1916; reprint, Gloucester, Mass.: Peter Smith 1959), 133.

ment, was Isaac Watts (1674–1748), who wrote about six-hundred hymns, the best known probably being "When I Survey the Wondrous Cross." John Newton (1725–1807) did come under the influence of John Wesley and George Whitefield and penned "Amazing Grace," "Glorious Things of Thee Are Spoken," and "How Sweet the Name of Jesus Sounds," among a fairly large collection. Then, one should not forget Fanny Crosby (1823–1915), the blind poetess to whom Ira Sankey, song leader for Dwight L. Moody, gave much credit for the success of their meetings. She wrote about nine-thousand gospel songs, more than anyone else in recorded Christian history. Among her best known compositions are "Safe in the Arms of Jesus," "To God Be the Glory," "Saved By Grace," "Draw Me Nearer," and "Rescue the Perishing." All of these composers had a unique ability to sing the reality of the Gospel message into the hearts of believers. We must never underestimate the power of hymnody as an apologetic for the Christian faith.

In Great Social Movements

Closely related to some of these revivals were great social movements that made an impact for Christ in the world and bettered the lot of humanity. And, of course, they provided an apologetic for the reality of the faith because it was their faith that impelled people to launch these efforts. As early as 1774 John Wesley "declared all slave-holding absolutely inconsistent with any kind of natural justice, let alone Christian ethics."[11] But the one who took the lead in the abolition of slavery in England was William Wilberforce (1759–1833). Associated with the Clapham Sect, a group of upper-class evangelicals, he and his friends sought to evangelize the upper classes as Wesley had been reaching the lower and middle classes of Great Britain. As a member of Parliament, he provided leadership

---

11 J. Edwin Orr, *The Eager Feet* (Chicago: Moody Press, 1975), 180.

for the abolitionist forces along with Thomas Clarkson, William Pitt, and John Newton (the hymn writer who had earlier been captain of a slaving ship). The Wesleyan movement provided the troops and solicited the signatures on petitions to Parliament. Wilberforce and his friends secured the abolition of the slave trade in 1807, and the complete abolition of slavery in England and the British Empire was achieved in 1833, just before Wilberforce's death. Wilberforce also played a leading part in the formation of the British and Foreign Bible Society (1804) and the Church Missionary Society (1799). He was once described as "the authorized interpreter of the national conscience" in England.

A tireless campaigner against slavery in the United States was the evangelist Charles G. Finney (1792–1875) who by his preaching is asserted to have made as many converts to the abolitionist cause as William Lloyd Garrison and his associates.

A younger contemporary of Wilberforce was Anthony Ashley Cooper, the Seventh Earl of Shaftesbury (1801–85). He entered Parliament in 1826 and after a couple of decades in the House of Commons entered the House of Lords. Shaftesbury spent his life as an evangelical social reformer. His experience with God led to a fierce concern for the elimination of social ills. He first tackled the problems of the mentally ill and was chairman of the Lunacy Commission from 1845 until his death. He secured the establishment of a Royal Commission of Inquiry into children's employment, helped pass legislation in 1864 and 1867 that regulated child and female labor, helped pass legislation in 1875 that protected children from being used as chimney sweeps. Between 1833 and 1847 Shaftesbury's main political concern was the factory system, and he helped pass the Ten Hours Act (1847) as well as the Factory Act (1874) to limit the hours of labor and improve the lot of workers in general. His tireless efforts led him also to work with the

London City Mission, the YMCA, The British and Foreign Bible Society, and the Church Missionary Society.[12]

The impact of Wesley's revivals in English society was so great that J. Wesley Bready argued that they saved England from the excesses suffered by the French in the days of the French Revolution. Bready developed and defended his argument in *England Before and after Wesley* and *This Freedom Whence?*

It is tempting to make comments about what we know of the desire of political leaders in contemporary American life to know God and serve Him. But it does not seem appropriate to name those on Capitol Hill who periodically hold prayer meetings in their House or Senate offices and who in various ways seek to bring their Christian experience to bear on public issues. In fairness to them, these should remain private matters, unless and until they choose to make them public. Perhaps it is sufficient to quote a printed and public statement made by Senator Mark O. Hatfield of Oregon and to let it speak for the rest. Long ago he took a stand that has guided him over the years:

> Following Jesus Christ has been an experience of increasing challenge, adventure, and happiness. How true are His words: "I am come that they might have life, and that they might have it more abundantly." It is not to a life of ease and mediocrity that Christ calls us, but to the disciple-like, Christ-empowered life. No matter what field we are in, we are called to give our complete allegiance to Him. No cause, noble as it may seem, can be satisfying or purposeful without the direction of Christ. I can say with all sincerity that living a committed Christian life is

12 The work of Wilberforce and Shaftesbury and other evangelicals concerned with the social ills of England is briefly told in Earle E. Cairns, *Saints and Society* (Chicago: Moody Press, 1960).

truly satisfying because it has given me true purpose and direction by serving not myself but Jesus Christ.[13]

Evidences there are aplenty that multitudes of Christians over the centuries have experienced God in a very real way. These experiences have motivated many in leadership roles to make a significant impact on society at large. But for all of us such experiences enable us to stand tall in the midst of adversity, give us courage to tackle the challenges of life, and provide us with peace and serenity in the midst of difficulty.

---

13 Merton B. Osborn, comp., *From Darkness to Light* (Chicago: Moody Press, 1962), 15. This statement first appeared in a tract published by the American Tract Society.

Chapter 9

CAN I APPRECIATE THE LIMITS OF CHRISTIAN APOLOGETICS?

We have tried to provide a brief defense of the Christian faith in the foregoing pages. Scholars often call this an exercise in apologetics or an apology, from the Greek word *apologia*, meaning a "defense." Such activity should not be confused with the popular concept of an apology, which has a negative connotation and involves an admission of error and often makes an excuse for unacceptable behavior. Here we are seeking to confirm, or affirm, the faith, not to prove it in the sense of arguing for its validity among all the philosophical alternatives. To confirm, or affirm, that the Bible and Christianity are what they claim to be is a very different exercise from arguing from open-ended suppositions to certain philosophical verities. The primary concern of the present chapter is to discover what apologetics, or Christian evidences, can or cannot do for us. In making this effort it might be most useful first to ask why apologetics have become necessary; second, what have apologists attempted; third, what have they accomplished;

and fourth, what is the value of apologetics to various publics today.

WHY APOLOGETICS HAVE BECOME NECESSARY

All through the Middle Ages, the West was officially Christian. This meant that in religious and political circles, in society at large, and in the mind of the layperson, the controlling intellectual viewpoint was that God did indeed exist, that He had revealed Himself in an infallible Bible, that Jesus Christ was the Virgin Born Son of God incarnate, that He died on the cross for our sins and rose again, and that He would some day return in judgment. People made their peace with God through the church and the sacraments; there was no general understanding of the need for a personal conversion experience. Even when the university system developed, especially in the thirteenth century, there was no abandonment of the faith. The dominant philosophical system of the Middle Ages was Scholasticism, which sought an intellectual certainty of the faith and a harmonization of faith and reason. In the hands of such giants as Thomas Aquinas, reason became a "handmaiden of theology." Judaism, too, maintained an orthodox stance, holding to a belief in a supernatural God who could perform miracles and to an inspired Bible (for them, the Old Testament).

Then, gradually, erosion took place. The Renaissance (c. 1300–1600) stressed a humanism and a critical spirit that introduced a wave of secularism but did not yet lead to alternatives to orthodox Christianity. The Reformation broke the iron grip of the Roman Catholic Church on Europe and opened the door to individual belief of one kind or another. Once a break from Rome had come, there was no way to prevent other breaks or to guarantee that any theological conformity could be maintained. A hint of things to come occurred with the activities of Faustus Socinus (1539–1604), the founder of Socinianism. Originally from Italy, Socinus spent most of his years teaching and preaching in Poland. There he espoused an anti-Trinitarian system, a rationalistic interpretation of Scripture, a separation of church and state, and a belief that Jesus was a man who lived a life of exemplary obedience to God and ultimately was deified. When the Polish parliament broke up his movement and banished his followers, many found their way to Holland and England, where they injected liberal influences into the theology of those two countries.

Coming along at the same time as the Renaissance and the Reformation, astronomy posed a special threat to the Christian way. Copernicus, in his *Revolution of the Heavenly Orbs* (1543, while Luther was still alive), taught that the universe revolved around the sun instead of the earth. Building on that, Descartes, in his *Discourse on Method* (1637), viewed the universe as unified and mathematically ordered, a perfect machine operating according to natural law. Newton, in his *Principia* (1687), postulated that this predictable machine operated as it did because of universal gravitation.

Of course there is nothing wrong with astronomy, and these men taught views now universally held, but some began to teach that nature was a *closed system* of causes and effects, ruled by universal and dependable laws. Although God was looked on as a first cause, necessary to set the system going, once He did so, He no longer interfered or intruded into the world of nature or humanity. Thus, miracle and providence were relegated to the ash heap. The greatest divine intrusion of all, the incarnation of Jesus Christ, presumably did not occur; Jesus became merely a wonderful person with a superior ethic. Divine intrusion in the form of inspiration and revelation did not occur either, and the Bible became merely a human book.

Enlightenment leaders of the eighteenth century get credit for advancing this religious viewpoint, known as deism. Deism spread across western Europe and became the dominant view of American intellectuals of the Revolutionary War generation, as a result of our alliance with France. The best known of the Enlightenment leaders, Voltaire (in France), laid the foundation for the "Higher Criticism" of Scripture in the nineteenth century in his impertinent, *Questions of Dr. Zapata*. On this foundation Julius Wellhausen and others (in Germany) erected the liberal, or higher-critical, system of biblical study that came to dominate in the West. Wellhausen, in his epochal *Prolegomena to The History of Ancient Israel* (1878), linked his nonsupernatural views of Scripture and Christianity in general to the increasingly popular evolutionary concepts of Charles Darwin. Although natural evolution had its beginnings among the Greeks in the sixth century B.C., Darwin popularized the philosophy in his *Origin of the Species* (1859) and *Descent of Man* (1871).

The new liberalism of the latter part of the nineteenth century and the early twentieth rested on the twin postulates of the denial of the supernatural and the evolution of religion and man. Thus, liberalism viewed the Bible as a human book put together by late editors from a collection of sources. Biblical miracles were explained away and predictive prophecy was eliminated (only partially successfully) by redating the prophecies so they would appear to be history. On the basis of the evolution of religion, the critics taught that religious views and practices advanced from no religion at all to an elevated monotheism. As a merely human book, the Bible was thought to be shot through with error. All this resulted in open warfare between orthodoxy and liberalism on both sides of the Atlantic late in the nineteenth century and early in the twentieth.

WHAT APOLOGISTS HAVE ATTEMPTED

In the face of all this attack, some have deliberately sought to defend the faith in this century, and others have inadvertently provided a confirmation of it. A doctrinal effort to combat the departure from conservative theology in America was the publication of a twelve-volume popular set called *The Fundamentals* (1910–12). Produced under the successive editorship of A. C. Dixon, Louis Meyer, and R. A. Torrey, these books especially upheld the Virgin Birth of Christ, His physical resurrection, the inerrancy of Scripture, the substitutionary atonement, and the imminent, physical second coming of Christ. Millions of copies were distributed free and served as a rallying point for the faith. Those who subscribed to the doctrines set forth in these books came to be known as "Fundamentalists." Counterattack against liberalism also took the form of the founding of scores of Bible institutes and Bible colleges to inculcate the faith.

Scholars who attacked higher criticism and rationalism appeared on both sides of the Atlantic late in the nineteenth century. Among the European scholars were E. W. Hengstenberg and Franz Delitzsch in Germany and Abraham Kuyper in Holland. The latter founded the Free University of Amsterdam, destined to become a great center of orthodoxy. On the American side of the Atlantic, Charles Hodge defended a supernaturally inspired Bible during his long tenure as professor of biblical literature and later of theology at Princeton Seminary (1820–78). A. A. Hodge ably succeeded his father at Princeton (1877–86). In 1887 B. B. Warfield followed Hodge as professor of theology at Princeton. At home in Hebrew, Greek, modern languages, theology, and biblical criticism, he staunchly defended an inerrant Scripture and cardinal evangelical doctrines in a score of books and numerous pamphlets. William Henry Green began a distinguished career at Princeton Seminary in 1851. Teaching Old Testament and Semitic studies, he administered telling blows against destructive higher criticism in his *General Introduction to the Old Testament* and *Higher Criticism of the Pentateuch.* In 1900, the scholarly Robert Dick Wilson joined the Princeton Old Testament faculty and argued forcefully for the conservative position in such works as *Scientific Investigation of the Old Testament* and *Studies in the Book of Daniel*. In 1906, J. Gresham Machen joined the Princeton New Testament faculty and produced such significant apologetic works as *Origin of Paul's Religion*, *Christianity and Liberalism*, and *The Virgin Birth of Christ*.

In 1929, when a liberal realignment occurred at Princeton, Machen and Wilson joined Oswald T. Allis, Cornelius Van Til, and others in founding Westminster Theological Seminary. Allis' *Five Books of Moses* was another apologetic for the conservative position. Cornelius Van Til launched a system of apologetics and published over twenty books during his teaching career. Perhaps his best known is *The Defense of the Faith*. Other scholars should be mentioned, but the purpose here is not to be exhaustive. We should note two other significant apologists, however: Gordon H. Clark and Edward John Carnell. Among Clark's important works are *A Christian View of Men and Things*. Of Carnell's nine books, *An Introduction to Christian Apologetics* is especially significant. Those who wish to pursue further some of the twentieth-century systems of apologetics in America will find Gordon R. Lewis's *Testing Christianity Truth Claims* (1976) to be helpful.

The number of those who have inadvertently provided a confirmation of the Scriptures or who have blunted the attacks of higher criticism during this century is far more numerous than those who have deliberately sought to establish an apologetic. This is certainly true in the fields of archaeology and Near Eastern studies. Pride of place in this group goes to W. F. Albright, "dean of biblical archaeologists," formerly of Johns Hopkins University. In a preface to an early edition of his *Archaeology of Palestine and the Bible,* he told how he had begun his career with a very low view of the Patriarchal narratives in Genesis but had himself contributed to the acceptance of them historically.

In the 1974 edition, he spoke of the "extraordinary accuracy of the narratives of the Patriarchs."[1] During his long and distinguished career, Albright demonstrated a remarkable honesty and flexibility in handling ancient Near Eastern data, going wherever the evidence led him and moving in an increasingly conservative direction. In his writings and his public lectures, he often attacked Wellhausen's basic tenets. Through his directing of doctoral studies and consultation with an untold number of authors in the field of biblical studies, he was able to moderate the theological position of many and to engender greater respect for the biblical text.

While Albright's contribution was primarily to Old Testament studies, Sir William M. Ramsay's was essentially to New Testament studies. Going to Asia Minor as a critic of Luke's accuracy in the narrative of Acts and even seeking to demonstrate Luke's untrustworthiness, he turned into an "evangelist" for Luke's accuracy and for the New Testament in general. Like Albright, he made a tremendous impact on a whole generation of scholars. Further comments on Ramsay appear in chapter 2.

Then, there is a host of scholars who have confirmed various aspects of biblical history. For example, there was Hugo Winckler, whose excavations at Bogazköy (east of Ankara) showed that the Hittites were a historical people after all. There were the excavators at Khorsabad (north of Nineveh) who dug up the palace of Sargon II of Assyria to demonstrate that this "fictitious" person had lived and ruled. There was Rassam's discovery of the Cyrus cylinder at Babylon that showed that the Persian king really did issue a decree for captive peoples to return to their homes (Ezra 1). There was the work of Yigal Shiloh in uncovering and evaluating the wall Nehemiah built in Jerusalem.

---

1 William F. Albright, *The Archaeology of Palestine and the Bible* (Cambridge, Mass.: American Schools of Oriental Research, 1974), 144.

Whole teams of scholars have worked on the Dead Sea Scrolls, demonstrating the remarkable degree of preservation of the Old Testament text and providing important information on biblical backgrounds. For example, the gospel of John, with its mention of the Logos in chapter 1, was thought by many to have been produced from a Hellenistic context. Now, as a result of studies in the Scrolls, it is believed to have a Palestinian Jewish context—as conservatives had believed all along. The Dead Sea Scrolls also raise questions about the late dates critics have assigned to some Old Testament books, e. g., Daniel.

Numerous scholars have also been working on the text of the New Testament all during this century. They have paid special attention to the papyri discovered in Egypt at the turn of the twentieth century and in subsequent decades (see chapter 2). They have shown that the New Testament text, like the text of the Old Testament, has been marvelously preserved over the centuries. In addition, they have demonstrated conclusively that the books of the New Testament were written during the first century and not during the second or third centuries, as critics used to charge. Therefore, the assertion that the view of Jesus as portrayed in the New Testament is a product of evolution over a period of generations and that the Gospels came into existence in the second or third centuries has been proven false. Critics generally are suggesting earlier and earlier dates for the composition of New Testament books.

WHAT APOLOGISTS HAVE ACCOMPLISHED

It is now time to summarize that which intentional or unintentional apologetic efforts have accomplished.

1. They have confirmed the essential historicity of the Bible. Albright asserted, "There can be no doubt that archaeology has confirmed the substantial historicity of Old Testament tradition."[2] Millar Burrows, formerly of Yale, observed more broadly, "On the whole, however, archae-

ological work has unquestionably strengthened confidence in the reliability of the Scriptural record. More than one archaeologist has found his respect for the Bible increased by the experience of excavation in Palestine."[3]

2.They have shown that many of the theories of higher critics of the Bible or their methods of interpreting Scripture were erroneous and should be discarded. Burrows has observed, "Archaeology has in many cases refuted the views of modern critics. It has shown in a number of instances that these views rest on false assumptions and unreal, artificial schemes of historical development. This is a real contribution, and not to be minimized."[4] William Hordern, former president of Lutheran Theological Seminary in Saskatoon, Saskatchewan, Canada, generalized: "It is now seen that Wellhausen was, to a large extent, rewriting history to fit Hegelian philosophy with its concept of evolutionary development."[5]

But Burrows warns: "It is quite untrue to say that all the theories of the critics have been overthrown by archaeological discoveries. It is even more untrue to say that the fundamental attitudes and methods of modern scientific criticism have been refuted."[6]

3. They have put the Bible in its background and setting and therefore made it more intelligible, more real, more believable.

4. They have helped to confirm and establish the text of the Bible. We are now in possession of enough facts to

---

2 William F. Albright, *Archaeology and the Religion of Israel*, 4th ed. (Baltimore: Johns Hopkins University Press, 1956), 176.

3 Millar Burrows, *What Mean These Stones?* (New York: Meridian, 1957), 1.

4 Ibid., 291–92.

5 William E. Hordern, *A Layman's Guide to Protestant Theology,* rev. ed. (London: Macmillan, 1968), 98.

6 Burrows, *What Mean These Stones?*, 292.

demonstrate that the Bible we love is essentially the message revealed to holy writers of old. We may conclude with Sir Frederic Kenyon, former director of the British Museum, that "the Christian can take the whole Bible in his hand and say without fear or hesitation that he holds in it the true word of God, handed down without essential loss from generation to generation throughout the centuries."[7]

THE VALUE OF APOLOGETICS
TO VARIOUS PUBLICS TODAY

Value to the Radical Critics

Critics may not have any interest in the field of apologetics; in fact they may resist its contributions. But they do so at the risk of quickly going out of date. G. Ernest Wright of Harvard in his Foreword to the 1974 edition of Albright's *Archaeology of Palestine and the Bible*, observed that Albright's "attack on Wellhausenism was a vigorous attempt to awaken Americans to the fact that they were seriously antiquated in Biblical matters." American scholars were unaware of the trends in German scholarship. There is constant movement, especially in the fields of archaeology and Near Eastern studies, in understanding and interpretation, that affects biblical study and makes the conservative position more respectable. Unfortunately, it is common to hear in college and high school classrooms attacks on the Christian faith that have been answered long ago.

Value to the Evangelical Student

Conservatives must keep in mind that while liberal critics may acknowledge the veracity of certain historical features of Scripture as a result of historical or archaeological investigation, they do not like to admit that this has any

_____

7   Frederic Kenyon, *Our Bible and the Ancient Manuscripts,* 5th ed. (New York: Harper, 1958), 55.

bearing on the supernatural element. An illustration of this fact is seen in McCown's attitude toward the biblical narrative of the fall of Jericho. After discussing the results of the excavations at the site he said, "The general dependability of the nonmiraculous features in the record is rendered probable."[8] In other words, he might be willing to accept the account of what happened, but he preferred to believe that the author of Joshua was mistaken as to the reason events transpired as they did (i. e., divine intervention). Burrows commented further on this matter:

> Much of what is said in the Bible, and that by far the most important part, cannot be tested by archeological evidence. That God is One, that he is Maker of heaven and earth, that man is made in his image, that Christ is the Incarnate Word of God, that by following him man finds eternal life, that the way to abundant life is the way of self-dedication and love—such teachings are entirely outside the sphere in which archeology or any science can have anything to say. Any attempt to demonstrate the truth of the Bible as revelation by an appeal to archeology necessarily proceeds on the false assumption that truth of one kind and truth of another kind must go together. In other words, it is taken for granted that if the historical record is accurate, the spiritual teaching also is reliable. . . . Religious truth is one thing; historical fact is another. Neither necessarily presupposes or accompanies the other.[9]

We must concede to Burrows that evangelicals have perhaps overemphasized the connection between the historical and theological elements of Sacred Writ and without question often have tried to prove too much. But the two

---

8 C. C. McCown, *The Ladder of Progress in Palestine* (New York: Harper, 1943), 81.

9 Burrows, *What Mean These Stones?*, 3–4.

elements do go together and must not be entirely divorced. Since it has been a trick of opponents of the Gospel to cast doubt on the theological message of the Bible by attacking its historical and scientific references, may we not conclude that the spiritual message is strengthened whenever some study demonstrates the veracity of the context of a theological dictum?

The last two quotations should help us realize that an apologetic may not be of great value when used on individuals educated in the liberal line of thought. In fact, the apologetic approach never has been very successful in winning avowed opponents of the truth. None of the Roman emperors was brought within the fold by the impassioned apologies addressed to them by the leaders of the early church. The two theological camps of the twentieth century—liberal and conservative—follow antithetical sets of postulates: the one nonsupernatural and the other supernatural. An apologetic can bring liberals to agreement only on historical features. It cannot cause them to reverse themselves on the issue of the supernatural. We do not mean to say, however, that such individuals are beyond the reach of the Gospel; certainly the Holy Spirit can woo them to the Son, even though all of our academic approaches may fail.

Value to the Unbeliever

There is a class of non-Christians with whom one may use an apologetic effectively. Those are individuals who are close to salvation but find that certain intellectual difficulties pose hurdles too great for them to leap. In that case, a few solutions may be offered from the fields of Near Eastern studies, or historical or philosophical apologetics in order to dispel the doubts, and the person might ultimately be brought to know the Lord through a witness begun in that way. Obviously it will be necessary for believers to be informed about such "solutions" in order for them to help unbelievers jump the "hurdles" and move into the circle of faith. The heart cannot delight in what the mind rejects as false.

Value to the Lay Believer

Apologetics perform their greatest ministry in the lives of lay believers, however. Such studies help them stand true to the faith in the classroom, where the attacks on all one holds dear are very great. Apologetics adds external factual support for the faith as doubts arise within the individual. Apologetics can strengthen believers in their activity in the world at large as they face the skeptical barbs of the literature they read, the television they watch, and the people with whom they come in contact. Moreover, in the process of persuading their pagan friends of the truth of the Christian faith, they may learn something about the underpinnings of their own belief. Apologetics is related to worship too. Adoration of God wells up in the soul when we see anew the adequacy and abiding quality of God's truth. If apologetics can do all that for believers, believers will do well to study the subject diligently.

FOR FURTHER READING

A whole library could be filled with books on apologetics or Christian evidences, and it seems almost presumptuous to attempt a bibliography on the subject. A proper bibliography probably should be organized by categories (e. g., miracles, resurrection) and perhaps should be annotated. Since this is a popular introduction to the subject, there is no attempt to develop such a bibliography, which might be found in a textbook. Rather, only a few titles are suggested for further reading. Though some are out of print, most should be available in libraries of Christian colleges or Bible institutes, or even church libraries. A few have made their way into community college and public libraries. Though a few are philosophical in nature (especially Swinburne's works), most are not and will not require a great deal of academic background. Of course additional books or articles appear in the footnotes.

Archer, Gleason L. *A Survey of Old Testament Introduction*. 3d ed. Chicago: Moody Press, 1994.

Brown, Colin. *Miracles and the Critical Mind*. Grand Rapids: Eerdmans, 1984.

Free, Joseph P. *Archaeology and Bible History.* Revised by Howard F. Vos. Grand Rapids: Zondervan, 1992.

Geisler, Norman L. The *Battle for the Resurrection.* Nashville: Thomas Nelson, 1989.

_____. *Miracles and Modern Thought.* Grand Rapids: Zondervan, 1982.

Hamilton, Floyd E. The *Basis of Christian Faith.* 3d ed. New York: Harper, 1946.

Lewis, C. S. *God in the Dock.* Grand Rapids: Eerdmans, 1970.

_____. *Mere Christianity.* New York: Macmillan, 1952.

_____. *Miracles.* New York: Macmillan, 1948.

Lewis, Gordon R. *Testing Christianity's Truth Claims.* Chicago: Moody Press, 1976.

McDowell, Josh. *Evidence that Demands a Verdict.* 2 vols. San Bernardino, Calif.: Here's Life Publishers, 1989.

Miethe, Terry L., ed. *Did Jesus Rise from the Dead?* San Francisco: Harper, 1987.

Morrison, Frank. *Who Moved the Stone?* Grand Rapids: Zondervan, 1976.

Pache, René. *The Inspiration and Authority of Scripture.* Chicago: Moody Press, 1969.

Pinnock, Clark H. *Set Forth Your Case.* Chicago: Moody Press, 1971.

Ramm, Bernard. *Protestant Christian Evidences.* Chicago: Moody Press, 1953.

Smart, Ninian. *Philosophers and Religious Truth.* London: SCM, 1964.

Swinburne, Richard. *The Concept of Miracle*. London: Macmillan, 1970.

_____. *The Existence of God.* Rev. ed. Oxford: Oxford University Press, 1992.

_____. Faith *and Reason*. Oxford: Oxford University Press, 1981.

Tenney, Merrill C. *The Reality of the Resurrection.* Chicago: Moody Press, 1972.

GENERAL INDEX

Abraham, 12–14, 16, 19
Adler, Mortimer, 141–42
Ahab, 29
Albright, William F., 15–16, 172–73, 175
Aquinas, Thomas, 136–37
archaeological apologetics, 42, 147, 167–68
Babylon, prophecy against, 56–58
British Museum, 29–33, 64, 66
Case, Shirley Jackson, 91
Crosby, Fanny, 162
Cyrus of Persia, return of Jews, 33
Dead Sea Scrolls, 44, 46, 173–74
Deism, 169–70
deity of Christ, 99–110
Door of Hope Mission, 156
Exodus from Egypt, 19
Finney, Charles G. 155, 160–61
Fundamentals, The, 171
Garstang, John, 24–25
Gaussen, Louis, 37–38
Glueck, Nelson, 27
God, existence of, 135–49
Gomorrah, destruction of, 8, 15–19
Gordon, Cyrus, 14
Haran, 13